THE **VC** WAY

THE **VC** WAY

Investment Secrets from the
Wizards of Venture Capital

JEFFREY ZYGMONT

PERSEUS PUBLISHING
Cambridge, Massachusetts

Copyright © 2001 by Jeffrey Zygmont

Cataloging-in-Publication Data is available from the Library of Congress
ISBN 0-7382-0387-4

Perseus Publishing is a member of the Perseus Books Group.

Find us on the World Wide Web at http://www.perseuspublishing.com

Perseus Publishing books are available at special discounts for bulk purchases in the U.S. by corporations, institutions, and other organizations. For more information, please contact the Special Markets Department at HarperCollins Publishers, 10 East 53rd Street, New York, NY 10022, or call 1-212-207-7528.

Text design by Jeff Williams
Set in 11-point Sabon by Perseus Publishing Services

First printing, February 2001

1 2 3 4 5 6 7 8 9 10—03 02 01

CONTENTS

To Madeleine,
whose abrupt arrival revitalized me.

ACKNOWLEDGEMENTS

Anyone who finds pleasure or profit here should first thank Perseus executive editor Jacqueline Murphy. Jacqueline conceived of a book that examines the ways successful venture capitalists invest. Next should come Kristen Wainwright of The Boston Literary Group, my agent. Kristen brought Jacqueline and me together, and then refereed as we refined the concept.

When writing any kind of book, you enter a period in which the intensity of the labor makes you a difficult companion for anyone forced to endure you. Therefore I am particularly grateful for my family's patience and support. That includes my wife, Donna, in particular, as well as my children—though at least Erik and Greta could escape to dorm rooms throughout much of this project. Madeleine, Greta's daughter, arrived while I was in the thick of composition. I expected her to be a sizeable interruption, until I rediscovered the revitalization you get from each goo of a cuddling infant. Madeleine turned out to be a helpful collaborator.

I learned about venture capital by interviewing a lot of venture capitalists, some entrepreneurs, and a few other specialists who operate inside or around the perimeter of venture capital. I feel indebted to all of these sources. But rather than call out their names here, I prefer to express my gratitude by accurately relaying the information and the insight they conveyed to me within the pages of the book. I hope they find themselves fairly represented.

INTRODUCTION—
AN ADVENTURE CAPITAL STORY

In July 2000, the Central Intelligence Agency opened offices at 2440 Sand Hill Road, a busy traffic feeder that runs northeastward out of the lolling foothills of the Santa Cruz Mountains. The road cuts between settlements of low-rise office buildings, it winks at a lavishly situated Episcopal church, skirts the Sharon Shopping Center, fronts a suburban apartment string, and nicks the upscale Stanford Mall just before it terminates at El Camino Real—the bustling central artery of California's Silicon Valley. The suite at 2440 Sand Hill Road is now home to the CIA's In-Q-Tel Inc. The name is meant to be a hip amalgam of the word "intelligence" and the character Q from the James Bond novels by Ian Fleming. Q is the wizard who outfits Bond with stealthy, high-tech gizmos that invariably foil the bad guys. Through In-Q-Tel, the CIA is branching into venture capital: investing in gizmos that, it hopes, will help it foil the bad guys.

With a pool of $34 million to distribute, In-Q-Tel looks for tiny, young companies developing advanced technologies that snug with the CIA's wants and needs. Of course, in exchange for its investment, In-Q-Tel takes a share of the new company, becoming a part owner. And it also gives the start-up some management advice to help ensure that each clever new idea will grow into a bona fide business. You see, not only does the CIA want to foster new spying technologies, it also would like its money back—along with a sizable investment return when it finally sells its ownership stake.

There's nothing new in that. The activities mimic the pattern that's very well established not just on Sand Hill Road but everywhere in Menlo Park, California, and all across Silicon Valley. It's called venture capital, and it goes on all over America. In fact, for just a minute disregard the distinction that In-Q-Tel's investment fund comes from the spy agency's coffers. And forget that any entrepreneur accepting an In-Q-Tel investment also takes the U.S. federal government as a distant partner (a condition that must make at least some free-thinking business founders pause). And finally, forget that government-backed operations find it awfully hard to escape purely political considerations that tilt toward favored people and government sanctioned concepts. If you overlook all those reasons why In-Q-Tel may not make unbiased investments based on the raw merits of the budding businesses it encounters, the CIA's participation in venture capital looks outright patriotic.

Venture capital as it's construed today—big money, bold risks, and, sometimes, staggering outcomes that change our entire culture—is quintessentially American. That's not just because it's practiced primarily and most successfully in the United States. (Other countries are scrambling to catch up, anyway.) Mostly it's because venture capital works best where clever kids with big ideas have the mobility to bust out and prove themselves. It operates most successfully where there is freedom to challenge the prevailing wisdom, the status quo, and the well-connected establishments that group thinking supports. Venture capital presupposes forward-looking social values that accept change as progress, that elevate improvement above tradition, and that remain optimistic about the future.

Mostly, venture capital works well in America because America lets it work without inhibitions. Venture capital is a dynamic and relentless change agent that challenges entrenched practices, attacks commercial power centers, and undermines the established order. Therefore, without necessarily meaning to be, venture capital is subversive. And subversion—changing the guard—is the founding principle of the United States.

But that all gets pretty lofty. And it's doubtful that the idea of subversion enters the thoughts of many venture capitalists. Certainly the CIA must have missed it.

Usually, of course, venture capital is undertaken as an investment. Specifically, it is an investment in a special asset class: new companies. But not just any new companies. Official statistics place something like 90 percent of all new starts as lifestyle businesses—which can pay off just fine for the hairdresser who wants to break out of Dot's Beauty Shop. But it is organized, institutional venture capital that looks after the other 10 percent: the companies and companies-to-be with a shot at rapid growth and high impact.

Overwhelmingly the budding businesses that venture supports are involved in new technology. There are exceptions, of course. But by far most venture investing occurs in breakthrough technologies because that's where the money is. Breakthrough technologies promise enormous returns, because they create new markets that aren't already dominated by powerful and entrenched megacorporations. There's room for a shiny, young upstart to make a name and make a fortune. The upstarts still threaten established companies, because the new markets may displace old ones that shelter the status quo players. In new markets born of new technologies, the paybacks can be spectacular because the value of start-up companies is at zero or very near zero. They have no place to go but up—or maybe out. It's this risk—the ever-present threat of failure—measured against the possibility of spectacular rewards that accounts for the investment techniques and principles of successful venture capitalists. This book is about their methods.

It's based on a very simple and straightforward formula for finding out what they do: Ask them. The methods, techniques, principles, and procedures represented here come from interviews with noteworthy venture capitalists. Naturally some are more noteworthy than others. The subjects who contributed their knowledge and experience to this book include some old hands and some young hotshots. They come from venture capital firms that have in one way or another distinguished themselves—through consistently excellent investments, long-standing prestige, meteoric success with Internet start-ups, or maybe just public notoriety. The sample is wide enough to be representative, but it slants toward the top-tier, successful VCs. After all, the aim is not to discover how just any venture capitalist invests. It is to report how the successful ones get that way. And stay that way.

This book also compares venture-investing rules and principles to general investing practices. The idea is to let general investors mine for insights that might help when they're putting together their own portfolios. Some of the tricks to picking new companies correspond very closely to considerations that, say, stock buyers can keep in mind. Other venture approaches don't map well at all outside the practice. After all, as special assets, infant companies demand some special considerations. The whole reason the venture industry exists at all is to answer the peculiar needs of aspiring but still fragile entrepreneurial businesses. If others could offhandedly dump money into them, they would, because there is much money to be made. But venture capital is active investing. The investor takes an inherently risky position—spanking new companies must clear an awful lot of hurdles—in anticipation of higher returns as compensation for the risk. But then he vigorously applies a lot of specialized resources to help assure the investment comes home. Those specialized resources are the things this book is about: leadership, wisdom, involvement, knowledge, persistence, adaptation, showmanship, balance, and daring.

If you want to ignore the context and cut straight to those nine principles, you can skip the rest of this chapter and Chapters Two and Three as well. The second part of the book, starting with Chapter Four, digs into the specifics of how winning venture capitalists invest.

But the principles of venture investing make the most sense inside the context of where they operate, and what they accomplish. Besides, the anecdotes and the accomplishments make a fascinating story. The entrepreneurs that the new-venture industry supports are America's Cinderellas and Cinderfellas: people who make it by merit and worth, not by privilege. And the VCs themselves—at least the ones running near the head of the pack or aspiring to—are very interesting folks in their own right. These are very bright people. They are hardworking. Venture capitalists like their jobs, and therefore when they talk about them they engage you fully.

What's more, they feel proud of their achievements, particularly their contributions to the technological foment of the last quarter century, which shows up today as the cultural phenomenon called the Internet. That pride is justified. By their role in building a large and active entrepreneurial class, venture capitalists are changing the world.

1

THE RULES OF
SAND HILL ROAD

You could tell the story of venture capital without ever leaving Sand Hill Road. Well, almost. The 1.5-mile stretch of Sand Hill in Menlo Park, roughly between Interstate 280 and Sharon Park Drive, is the spiritual center of the industry. Its clusters of casual, comfortably spaced, automobile-age office buildings—low-slanting roofs topped with cedar shingles—house what has to be the world's greatest concentration of venture capitalists, including many of the most celebrated firms. They include Kleiner Perkins Caufield & Byers, at 2750 Sand Hill. That name means venture capital to people who pay even passing attention to the trade. Benchmark Capital occupies 2480 Sand Hill. Canaan Partners has offices at 2884. Matrix Partners, an east coast–west coast bicoastal firm, is at 2500. Mohr Davidow Ventures resides at 2775. Redpoint Ventures and Sequoia Capital fill suites at the 3000 Sand Hill complex. Throw in the others and you end up with so many venture practices on Sand Hill Road that some firms make a point to locate elsewhere. "I don't believe eagles flock," flips Ann Winblad, who cofounded Hummer Winblad Venture Partners in 1989. Hummer Winblad headquarters itself in San Francisco—a city that supports a respectable flock of VCs itself. Her office, shadowed by the Bay Bridge, sits in a neighborhood that's going tony fast. Stylish offices are filling space once occupied by warehouses and workshops, while street-level storefronts change over to slick bistros straining to look chatty and inviting.

Sand Hill Road angles more or less into the center of Silicon Valley, where the most spectacular contemporary successes of venture investing occur. Building on the momentum that began with the come-on of computer chips in the 1960s, followed by the development of all the technologies like software and instrumentation and communications that rely on intelligent silicon, the Valley today has become the hub of the Internet. The Internet, along with its hyper-linked extension of pictorial information centers called the World Wide Web, is a combined computing and communication medium that is so pervasive and so unprecedented that it creates a lot of the new markets that venture capital thrives upon. And it has certainly thrived. Since Internet and Web technology began their acceleration in the middle 1990s, venture capital has grown with blind abandon. In 1999, more than $46 billion was entrusted to venture capitalists to place on upstart companies. In 1995, just over $8 billion was infused into the industry.

Conspicuous investing explains the popular notoriety that venture capital started attracting in the late nineties. New-venture firms not only made some spectacular sums by investing in Internet start-ups; by so actively pushing the technologies that comprise the information superhighway, they also played a pivotal role in building this significant new network. That made people notice what had once been a small and obscure investment community.

Consequently, on Sand Hill and in Silicon Valley today, the wheedling that goes on around the venture capital industry has reached such proportions that at times it can seem like a parody of itself, inspiring circus-quality stunts that anticipate a kind of *Price Is Right* giveaway of get-started money.

On May 12, 2000, two hopeful young men sat on folding chairs on a median strip on Sand Hill Road, just before it crosses over

I–280. They held a poster board sign advertising: WILL WORK FOR SEED MONEY. They wanted a mere $500,000 to help them launch Ad-Pad Inc., their idea for an electronic game company that college students would visit on the Web. To lure them to the site, Ad-Pad planned to give away prizes like CDs and other tchotchkes beloved by the university crowd. "College kids love free stuff," Seth Karm beamed assuredly. Karm is one half of the partnership and, officially, director of business development. He explained that, to earn its keep, Ad-Pad would sell advertising space interspersed among its games. By noon, the in-your-face gimmick had earned about a half-dozen inquiries, shouted from cars stopped at the traffic light beside the beggars' outpost.

Of course, Sand Hill Road is only the symbolic center. Venture capital goes on all over the place. A sizable satellite operates on the coast opposite Silicon Valley: in and around Boston. In fact, through much of the 1970s and 1980s, the suburban territory known unimaginatively as Route 128—named for the freeway that loops around Boston in a wide half-circle—challenged the Valley as the premier home of high technology. New York, the city, home of old-industry tycoons and establishment high finance, performs its share of nimble, new-venture activities, giving rise to a community of entrepreneurial concerns called Silicon Alley. The city of Austin, state capital of Texas, wins notice as an active venture center. Other concentrations of greater or lesser note come up. In 1993, Steven Stull even struck on the idea of practicing venture capital deliberately in areas outside of the entrepreneurial mainstream. He based his Advantage Capital Partners in New Orleans, with operations in St. Louis, Tampa, and, most recently, in New York City to serve the Northeast region. "Our strategy from the beginning was to locate in areas that are under-served by the venture-capital industry, so that we don't compete with hundreds of other firms looking at the same transaction," says Stull.

Of course, venturers don't invest only in their own backyards, although some of the Silicon Valley firms find business enough in the neighborhood. Draper Fisher Jurvetson set up in a harbor-side complex in Redwood City—with brawny shippers of bulk freights as neighbors on the flats that run out into the lower San Francisco Bay—so that the firm would be close to Highway 101. "Most of our companies are either just south of here or north of here off of 101," explains John Fisher, a cofounder. Considering the amount of time a VC spends giving hands-on assistance to a holding after its investment, a freeway ramp can become a strategic asset.

Yet geography matters not a jot next to the position venture capital occupies in business and, beyond that, across the entire cultural landscape.

Venture capital is the place where ambitious people can go to pursue their ideas—for the ideas venture capitalists judge valuable. Yes, it bankrolls their businesses with needed cash. But just as important as the money it doles out—in increments amounting to millions and tens of millions at a time—is the support venture capital provides to entrepreneurs. That includes tangible elements of support, like coaching in essential business practices, recruiting seasoned and compatible executives, brainstorming high-level strategy moves, and granting admission to a well-established network of connections that includes potential partners, future investors and underwriters, recruiters, accountants, lawyers, and vital co-entrepreneurs.

But above even that comes an intangible, essential contribution of venture capital: It creates the very cultural mind-set that encourages talented people to start new businesses, because they recognize there is a system out there set up to enable them to do it. The system is set up to help and support and encourage them. A venture capitalist doesn't care who you are or where you come from. He'll open his arms if you have an idea that looks like it can be turned into a sustainable business that will pay him back in spades for the money and the effort he contributes to it. It is the democratization of capital: The most valuable ideas win, regardless of to whom they're attached.

The VC system of small-business creation provides an entrepreneurial safe haven, a clearly demarcated pocket within the economy where small, fledgling companies are accepted, encouraged, and understood. Venture capital has created an environment in which innovation, determination, and relentless toil are encouraged by the promise of commercial rewards. Personal rewards, too. That's important to entrepreneurs. The people who start new companies are ambitious high-achievers by nature. Rather than do it for someone else, they want to do it themselves, venturing out to stamp their inventions with their own signatures. If not, they would remain inside the big corporations. Or after earning technical degrees or MBAs from high-flying schools like Stanford University and the Massachusetts Institute of Technology, more bright young minds would surrender to a predictable wage and a time card. After all, who has the courage to set up shop solo, shouldering on their own all the duties and responsibilities of building a company? Who has the experience and the expertise to tackle all the various tasks it demands, like attracting and hiring good people, sweating out the intricacies of bending a technical insight into a usable product, coaxing consumers to buy a new concept they may not have even dreamed about? Who has the money?

It wouldn't even occur to ambitious, capable people to parlay their ideas into vibrant new businesses if they didn't have a place to take their ambitions. At least it wouldn't occur to nearly as many. And an awful lot of those few who tried it would smack against barriers they couldn't surmount. The business of venture capital is to clear away those barriers.

"The VCs are there to build a company," says Bryan Stolle, a star entrepreneur who has seen the system succeed and has seen it fail. He is cofounder and chief executive of Agile Software, a six-year-old, venture-sponsored company that still makes eyes twinkle in the Valley. "They understand the process. So when you don't hit your numbers, it's not a big deal. That doesn't mean that they don't hold you accountable, but they understand that it happens. When products take six months longer or eight months longer to develop than you thought, they don't freak out over it. When you're still struggling to figure out where the market is, they understand all that stuff."

Of course, technical innovation and the change it engenders also come out of the corporate establishment. Intel never fails to wring more magic out of silicon, creating microprocessors with more and more computing capabilities. Even Ford—called an old-economy company not only because it predates the Internet but because it actually bends metal—made some pioneering advances in speech technology, enabling computers to carry on conversations with people. It had to, to help drivers stay in their lanes while operating mobile equipment like cell phones and navigation systems.

But entrepreneurs goose the process. For one thing, they operate outside of the stifling corporate bureaucracies, the rigid hierarchies, and the self-preserving command chains that can smother innovation. Before he started Agile Software, Bryan Stolle tried to sell his product concept to the corporate brass at an outfit called Sherpa, where Stolle was a marketing executive. Sherpa itself had been an entrepreneurial beginner not many years before, so it's not like Stolle was lost inside IBM or General Motors. Still, says Stolle, "I spent a good six months trying. I had been there seven years and I felt a lot of loyalty to the company. But you just reach the point where you've beat your head against the wall too many times. The inertia is like a big flywheel going in one direction. We're so enslaved to our customer base that we can't go off and do something different."

Even when they're specifically assigned to do something different, thinkers inside Big Incorporated can have a hard time getting their thoughts above ground. Consider the famous example of the graphical user interface for computers. Computer people call it by its acronym, GUI, which they pronounce as *gewey*, as if that simplifies it. Whatever its name, a GUI isn't so much a discrete technology. It's the concept of controlling a computer by pointing to and selecting representative symbols on the screen. The concept originated at the Palo Alto Research Center of Xerox Corp. But it took Apple Computer Corp. to put the idea to work. As the story goes, Apple cofounder Steve Jobs smuggled out the concept in his noggin during a 1979 tour of the center. Apple at the time was just a tenuous start-up, living on venture funding from Sequoia Capital and Venrock Associates, a New York firm started by Laurance Rocke-feller in the 1930s to wager some of the family's oil money. Sure, Jobs gets roundly slammed for the theft. But Xerox and its Palo Alto Research Center also get chided for their habit of sitting on brilliant innovations. If it was left to them, who knows when the idea may have seeped into widespread use. Yet it's an important idea. The graphical user interface makes computers much simpler to use than the alternative, which is to type in arcane commands in oddly structured computer diction. As computers have become more accessible and accommodating, people have come to feel more eager to buy and use them. This expanding, enthusiastic mar-ket in turn encourages computer makers to develop even better computers. It also provides the cash they need to fund the develop-ment.

Therefore, you can easily argue that without a GUI, the market for personal computers would have developed much slower, be-cause people would have had a harder time making them work. A smaller, slower-growing market would have slowed down the de-velopment of PC technology itself. In other words, without Jobs's early commercialization of the graphical user interface, both com-merce and contemporary society wouldn't yet be enjoying the com-monplace benefits of personal computers, which have increased business productivity and enriched personal lives. Would PCs have gotten there eventually? Probably. But the point is that they're here now, and that clears the decks for subsequent improvements in who knows what areas.

By and large the R&D spending of big companies is survival money. They exist to sell products, and they'll improve their prod-ucts to the extent they need to in order to keep their customers buy-ing them. That's hardly a formula for blinding innovation.

"Large companies that have momentum and a track record within a certain field of operation need to maintain their focus on the management of their processes," observes David Malfera, an entrepreneur who has ginned along a fair bit of innovation in the telecommunications trade. "What they don't need to do is squander resources on a number of research and development ideas that may or may not work. Their structure penalizes entrepreneurial thought. What is rewarded is competitive, consistent performance."

On the other hand, Big Inc. will often purchase entrepreneurial thought to keep a technical edge. A lot of venture investments get cashed out when precocious small companies are picked up as acquisitions by industry-leading behemoths. In exchange for their ownership stake in the start-up, the private investors get the more valuable stock of the well-established public company that makes the purchase.

"It's an entrepreneur's job to cultivate concepts and ideas into a valid business," says Malfera. "When he can develop a concept that works, when he can substantiate the benefit of the concept, he can sell that idea or sell that business line to a more mature company that will not take the initial risk to develop the technology."

But it isn't always just an aversion to risk-taking that can cause muscular corporations to hold back innovation, either. An entrenched enterprise usually doesn't have much incentive to change the world, because it has so much staked in the world as it is presently ordered. In fact, an established business typically feels much greater incentive to leave affairs the way they are. They already own their market, or at least a profitable chunk of it, and they have a lot of capital tied up in making products the way they're currently constructed. It gets expensive to change things. It is costly to reengineer products, to reequip manufacturing plants, to reorient sales teams, and to reeducate consumers.

For example, advances arrived a lot more slowly back when telecommunications services were monopolized by Ma Bell and some lesser siblings, together couching comfortably behind government regulations that kept out any competition. "They managed the introduction of new technology to suit what was clearly a lengthy period for depreciation of capital equipment," charges Jim Hynes, a VC who made a lot of hay investing in telecom after deregulation opened the industry to competition. Before he became a venture capitalist, Hynes had been a Bell customer on a grand scale, as the executive in charge of telecommunications for Chase Manhattan Bank.

"When they weren't threatened by somebody who could offer a competitive service based on new technology, there wasn't a great deal of urgency for them to throw everything out just so they'd be able to provide something new," Hynes observes. "Because of their embedded investment, they would manage the delivery of new technology on a schedule, frequently stifling certain things that could have been used earlier."

Think of it as big-business inertia. It leaves it to the entrepreneur to change the world—or at least a tiny corner of it. The entrepreneur has no other choice. Unlike any larger rivals, his new company has no history to protect. What's more, if his product doesn't change things for the better by offering something more than the current crop, he'll never sell it. He'll fail.

Change is his only hope.

"The entrepreneur believes so strongly in an idea that he is willing to put all his time and his personal wealth at risk to develop it," says Malfera. He speaks from experience. In 1983, he secured bank loans to start Pace Long Distance Service, one of the early, competitive inter-exchange carriers that ventured out to hunt giants. Its weapon was the single-price long-distance rate that is commonplace today. Back then, the established players in long distance charged according to how far a call went. The new guys couldn't do that, says Malfera. "When competitors came into the market, they needed some way of differentiating their services. What was born was the postalized long-distance rate." The idea is so appealing that eventually even Goliaths like AT&T had to offer it.

By the way, Malfera has also seen big-business R&D from the inside. He was an engineering vice president at National Computer Corp., and a telecommunications technical adviser at Honeywell Information Systems. As a senior engineer at GTE Telenet, he designed large-scale data-communications networks for Fortune 500 companies. Currently Malfera is president of Z-tel Network Services, part of a Tampa-based, integrated communications provider, which conveniently links together services like paging, Internet access, and regular telephony. Is it entrepreneurial? Z-tel was set up only in January 1998, with help from Acorn Ventures and Sewanee Ventures.

There are a lot more people like Malfera running around out there. Evan Schumacher went seeking venture aid in 1998 to jumpstart his software company Celarix. (He found it aplenty.) Some of his motives for joining the entrepreneurial class: "I want to build a sustainable part of the American economy. I want to create a workplace where people are respected, a workplace that challenges them, allows them to grow and reap all the professional, social, financial rewards of the experience." Schumacher is thirty-one. Nothing in his tone or demeanor would tempt you to doubt his sincerity. Celarix uses the Internet to deliver software services to the transportation industry. Schumacher selected transportation for his adventure first because it's his professional background. Secondly, he figures it's a place where he can make a big dent. He cites: "Transportation is the second largest industry and ten percent [of] the world's gross domestic product. It's the third oldest industry in the world"—which puts it two behind prostitution. "It's a market that can be changed forever, and we can be a catalyst to that. If I wanted to make $20 million in six months, we would have sold our company after we did our first round of financing." Instead, Schumacher, his cofounders, and venture investors are piloting Celarix toward an initial public stock offering. They want it to be around for a while.

That's not to say personal wealth isn't also a big motive behind entrepreneurial membership. It's like the trophy at the end of the race. "Venture capital inserts a profit motive into technology transfer," opines Oliver Curme, who has labored as a VC at Battery Ventures since 1985. "The idea is to develop new technologies and then transfer them out of the laboratories and into business, where they can have an impact on the economy. Twenty years ago, that was solely a function of corporate R&D labs. The corporate R&D labs were very inefficient. They've always been inefficient," says Curme, though he nevertheless gives them their due, noting that a lot of significant advances, like transistors, came out of corporate development. Besides, his own dad worked for thirty-five years in research for Eastman Kodak. But Curme's point is that highly motivated private development significantly increases the pace, magnitude, and volume of new thoughts. "We have a lot of really smart young people out there on the front lines, looking at technologies [that have] come along and anticipating how they can be applied to really shake the economy. It's the capitalist approach to R&D, where guys with a profit motive are out there trying to make money, and almost as a by-product they're benefiting society by making new technologies."

Whatever moves them to create, entrepreneurs are society's change agents. They improve the tools people use. The arrival of one-price postal-style rates may not cure cancer, but it brought a far sight more efficiency to long-distance service—which became a vitally important contribution a decade after 1983, when that new thing called the Internet started to clog communications lines. Besides, when consumers spend less money to talk New York to California, the capital is freed up to spend other ways, perhaps on fighting cancer. Economists call the process "wealth creation."

The technology mill touches everywhere, typically producing small changes that, in aggregate, keep culture moving forward. No power is immune from it. Whole commercial enterprises fall beneath turns of the technology cycle. Even onetime entrepreneurs get gobbled up if they don't flex with the changes. In the middle 1960s, computing pioneer Dr. An Wang started the company Wang Laboratories. It more or less created word processing. For a while that made it the premier name in office computing. But who's even heard of Wang today? Computing shifted to PCs, or general-purpose machines that can perform word processing but also run a myriad of other software titles, everything from games to spreadsheets and accounting programs. But Wang didn't change fast enough. It was stuck selling special-purpose, proprietary computers that couldn't use these whole new libraries of software available to general-purpose PCs. Its sales dried up, and the company shriveled.

And the cycle keeps churning. Mighty Microsoft benefited most from the movement to general-purpose computing: The market chose its software, the DOS and then Windows operating systems, as the common foundation that would support all those mix-and-match software titles. But that good fortune doesn't insulate it against the next cycle. Microsoft's biggest threat today is not the U.S. Justice Department, no matter how stridently federal prosecutors press their arguments that the Redmond company is a deceitful bully that smothers innovation outside of its walls. While the appeals process drags on and lawyers still wrangle over that accusation, the seductive Internet threatens to bring Microsoft to its knees. The Internet has simply changed the paradigm of personal computing. Not long ago, everyone who wanted their PCs to work and play together needed to run them on the same operating system—Microsoft's Windows, as it worked out. But to join the world today, all a PC must do is incorporate Internet standards. That liberating development eliminates the necessity for conformity with Windows.

Microsoft's comeuppance likely won't come quickly. Colossi have a long way to fall before they finally reach the ground. It's taken General Motors more than two decades to migrate from the world's most influential carmaker, responsible for half of the new cars purchased in the United States in the 1980s, to a bungling follower that struggles to assert any relevance in the auto world. Today its seven vehicle brands account for just over a quarter of new-car sales. Whither Microsoft? Now that the technological conditions that favored the company have shifted, it's inevitable that better minds will devise better alternatives to Windows, better word processing software than Word, and so on.

In fact, the entrepreneurial tussle that's building the Internet has already bred at least one serious rival to Microsoft's crown-jewel Windows. A software system called Linux, prized as a foundation that companies can use to support Web services, is being popularized by Red Hat Software. Red Hat was started in 1995 by Robert Young, an experienced small-businessperson, and Mark Ewing, a fresh-from-college programmer who brought some order to unruly versions of Linux that were beaming around the Internet. In 1998, Red Hat received equity investments from Benchmark Capital and Greylock, two of the most respected name brands in venture capital.

In fact, the Internet as a whole owes a lot to venture capital for its breakneck development and commercialization. Recognizing it as fertile but unplowed ground—the best territory for new companies to cultivate—venturers are behind the Internet as they've never backed a technology before. The raw investment figures get cited frequently in efforts to stagger and impress. But it's tough for many people to personally relate to a number like $75 billion, the amount that venture firms stoked into Internet-related businesses in 2000, according to Venture Economics and the National Venture Capital Association. You can get a better idea of the influence of venture capital by considering some of the seedlings it sponsored that have quickly grown into corporate entities that seem so well established, you'd swear they've been around as long as GM. Like Cisco Systems, the communications hardware maker. And Amazon.com, the on-line bookstore that's morphing into a retailer of, it seems, just about everything.

Could the company founders have done it without venture capital? Tom Monaghan started Domino's from a single storefront in Ypsilanti, Michigan, in 1960. After trading a VW Beetle for his brother's half of the business, he built the chain pizza by pizza. Monaghan even applied some innovation to the pizza-schlepping trade: He set up commissaries to prepare and deliver component ingredients for all the Domino's in a region, bringing economies of scale to what had been a one-pie-at-a-time, mom-and-pop industry.

Companies in the tech trades can also make it without venture support. Don't forget Malfera's incursions into telecommunications, funded by bank loans. Wang Laboratories, quite a highflier before it lost its way, skipped directly to a public offering to take advantage of an enthusiastic stock market. In his book *Greylock: An Adventure Capital Story*, William Elfers, Greylock's founding partner, tells how he was putting together a private-equity deal for Dr. Wang at the time. But he advised Wang to go the public route instead. The company could simply raise a lot more money that way. In acknowledgment, Dr. Wang made room for Greylock to buy some shares of the offering, over the objections of the investment bankers underwriting the Initial Public Offering (IPO).

More recently, venture veteran Jacqueline Morby, managing director at TA Associates, made repeated calls on the software company i2 Technologies, which sells what's called "enterprise software" that corporations use to help manage complex business operations. But like Wang, i2 never experienced the need to take a venture partner. In 1996, the high-flying software supplier went public without ever taking any institutional private-equity funding.

So venture funding isn't essential for start-up stardom. But there is also evidence that entrepreneurs who stay outside of the venture fold can encounter an inhospitable environment. The meteoric rise and spectacular crash of Toysmart.com is one example. Professional Web watchers once placed it among the most promising online retailers, partly for its policy of selling only kinder, gentler playthings—no plastic guns or arch-villain action figures. Patricia Seybold, a popular consultant who benefits as much as anyone in her business from people's short memories, even named it to her list of top five retailing sites.

Toysmart was actually an entrepreneurial relaunch of the established private company Holt Educational Outlet. David Lord, Toysmart CEO, teamed with a partner to buy Holt. They renamed it, and dashed into Web retailing.

Like Web start-ups everywhere, Toysmart needed funding fast to jump-start its operations, and for the carpet-bombing advertising that at the time was deemed necessary to create instant customer awareness—before a competing Web store could implant its name into the cultural consciousness. But Lord passed up $25 million offered by venture capitalists. Instead, he climbed into bed with the Walt Disney Co., ceding the Mouse 60 percent ownership in Toysmart for the same $25 million cash the venturers had offered, plus some advertising commitments. The decision seems reasonable. What better partner could a toy seller have than the friendly, furry rodent?

Nine months after the deal closed in August 1999, the marriage ended and Toysmart became "one of the first high-profile casualties of the Web-retailing shakeout," as *Wall Street Journal* reporter William Bulkeley wrote in an account published June 7, 2000. There's no question that Toysmart's failure stemmed partially from the singeing competition that plagued other promising start-ups in on-line consumer sales. It suffered the bad fortune to enter a market that Amazon.com also had staked out. Amazon.com launched its toy-selling segment in time for the 1999 holiday season and thereby stole a lot of thunder from Toysmart. Meanwhile, another competitor, eToys, managed to build much of the brand awareness that Toysmart eagerly sought. And if all that wasn't enough, well, Web retailing overall just failed to take off quite as fast and far as a lot of pundits once predicted.

But Lord complains that many of his company's problems grew from the fact that Disney just didn't get it: Its slow-moving, big-business practices and policies proved simply incompatible with the quick thinking and fast acting required of an entrepreneurial enterprise. Consequently, as Lord told the *Wall Street Journal*'s Bulkeley, Toysmart got a late start in prime selling seasons because of Disney foot-dragging before the deal could be signed and the cash turned over. Disney second-guessed and gummed up Toysmart's advertising plans. It over-scrutinized tie-ins between Mickey's powerful brands and Toysmart. Disney also kept changing its mind about Internet retailing strategy, while it reassigned executives in charge of it. That made it hard for Toysmart to even find an ear within the large, cumbersome company. Eventually it backed away from general merchandise entirely, concentrating on sales of Disney brands alone. The change left Toysmart marooned.

Certainly Mickey and his company have their side to tell, but it's clear that David Lord feels that Toysmart was ill served by its pop-icon corporate partner.

With their overriding aim to create successful businesses—in order to claim a return for the dough they sink into them—venture capitalists bring urgency and acceleration to new companies. That's vital. As a rule, modern technology markets reward speed more than they reward patience. They change so quickly. New products and new approaches have only a short life span before they're rendered obsolete by subsequent, hot new ideas. If the tinkerers and the idea-people don't get out their latest and greatest very fast, they are very likely to be leapfrogged. Whether it's goods or services, whether consumer gadgets, computer technology, communication equipment, medical meters, or you name it, if it's a product of high technology, its creator usually can't take a conservative, go-slow approach to putting it under the nose of shoppers. He doesn't have time to build up cash-flow sale by sale, expanding the business out-of-pocket as revenues grow enough to support, say, increased manufacturing, more R&D, wider distribution, additional advertising, or international sales. By the time he gets there, his buyers are likely to be agog over some latest innovation that makes his look quaintly dated.

As much as they need the cash to jump-start and sustain their early operations, and as much as they need the rub-off of business savvy from VCs who know the start-up game intimately, entrepreneurs also need a filter for their ideas—though relatively few want one, because few can actually make it through the mesh. In the competitive, quick-changing technology markets, many ideas are out of date before they're even afloat. Many are competing with so many similar ideas that are swimming in the same direction that they don't have a chance to make a big splash. A lot of ideas are just plain daft. Certainly the entrepreneur who dreams up a proposal isn't in the best position to judge. He loves the idea, which is why he's willing to stake huge chunks of his time, his creativity, his energy, his reputation, and even his personal fortune, whether little or big, on the concept. If an entrepreneur could command or cajole the money-granting authority, he'd have his idea promoted for the sheer beauty he sees in the stationery his business plan is printed on.

In 1999, Battery Ventures picked twenty winners out of the 10,000 deals it looked at. Draper Fisher Jurvetson cofounder John Fisher reports that 15,000 to 20,000 new business plans fill the firm's mailbags and e-mail boxes each year. Other high-profile venture outfits receive at least as many—though a lot are the same ones, as entrepreneurs make the rounds. As the VCs filter these they bring a measure of objective focus to the selection process: Will anybody want this thing? Will it make it in the marketplace? Their choices are rooted in a fiscal discipline, since they have to make money on the concepts they back. To make money, a concept has to offer enough to bring people to the store to buy it. In the end, the wide-open market decides which new ideas are worthy and which fall short. Venture capitalists work in advance of that, trying to pick the best among the unstratified mob that's clamoring to get space on the shelves.

Not that the venture backers get it right all the time. Anecdotally, it's generally accepted that only about two out of every ten deals pay off big. A lot of the remaining eight may come back winners, but not the megawinners that can get a venture capitalists enshrined in business lore.

Even their immunity from failure during the go-go era of Internet investing proved only temporary. For all the venture money pushed into e-commerce Web sites selling to consumers—the so-called business-to-consumer, or B2C sector, which was flooded with people eager to emulate the stunning notoriety of Amazon.com—failures began to grow conspicuous early in 2000, which was the moment the market for new companies was officially pronounced dry. Boo.com, a high-fashion, high-flying site for selling women's clothing, made news for its ability to burn through investors' cash. Conceived in mid-1998, Boo started selling on-line in late 1999. In May 2000, liquidators shut down the company. It had no hope of going public, since the IPO market had chilled to on-line retailers a couple of months earlier. In total, $135 million in private investments essentially vanished. Some came from venture-capital professionals, including San Francisco's 21st Century Internet Venture Partners, a firm that brandished its Web expertise. But a lot came from investment banks and private investors. According to reports, one bought into Boo after seeing its founders on the cover of *Fortune* magazine, which labeled Boo a "cool company."

Just as venture has its failures, it also has its detractors. People who play in the start-up segment bandy about the term "vulture capitalist." The logism is meant to suggest that these specialty investors prey on small companies. A vulture capitalist robs ownership and control from the founders and then picks the company clean, eventually abandoning the corpse if business turns badly, or, if it goes well, fattening themselves on the value of a company built by others.

Even some venture capitalists squirm a little at the popular image. To account for the label "vulture capitalist," one VC recites an assertion attributed to Donald Valentine: *I own the desk.* In 1972, Valentine founded Sequoia Capital, a Sand Hill Road resident that makes everybody's list of leading venture firms. His colleagues know him as opinionated, outspoken, iconoclastic, and exceedingly successful. Valentine was an early backer of Apple Computer, Oracle, and Cisco Systems, to name only three. His claim to "own the desk" applied to Cisco. He ran the company, he meant, by virtue of Sequoia's early, supporting investment. Valentine's partnership put in the initial $2.5 million start-up cash back in 1984, when Stanford University computer scientists Len Bosack and Sandy Lerner, along with a handful of other founders, started Cisco with a better idea for routing computer data. According to the common industry practice, Sequoia's investment gave Valentine a seat on the company's board of directors. In 1988 he became chairman of the board. As the legend goes, that same year he effectively fired Cisco's founders, bringing in his own management team under president and chief executive John

Morgridge. It's the sort of bold move that can make any entrepreneur queasy about shaking hands with a VC.

They'll find plenty of detailed and well-documented accounts to support their uneasiness. Izhar Armony—once an Israeli army tank commander, now a venture investor in the firm Charles River Partners—notices that the 1999 book *High Stakes, No Prisoners: A Winners Tale of Greed and Glory in the Internet Wars* makes the rounds among many entrepreneurs he encounters. It prepares them for a fleecing. *High Stakes, No Prisoners* is a first-person account of the speedy and stellar rise of Vermeer Technologies, told by its founder, Charles Ferguson. Vermeer was one of the early successes of the Internet age, and was started in 1994 around Ferguson's idea for selling easy-to-use software that helps people build Web sites. Microsoft acquired Vermeer very early in 1996 for $130 million. Its Web site–building software, called FrontPage, helped Microsoft jump-start its once-lagging presence in Web and Internet technology.

A large part of Ferguson's tale centers on his battles with his venture funders, especially with Andy Marcuvitz of Matrix Partners. Matrix was one of three backers that collectively took 50.1 percent of Vermeer in a first-round funding deal that closed in January 1995, eight months after Ferguson started the company with partner Randy Forgaard, an MIT-educated computer scientist. Both Matrix and Sigma Partners kicked in $1.6 million. Atlas Venture, a firm that operates out of Boston and Menlo Park, put in $800,000, taking only a non-voting, observer's seat on the Vermeer board of directors.

In *High Stakes, No Prisoners,* Ferguson complains loudly about the ardors of first winning any attention from VCs, and then of putting together a deal he could accept, and then of arranging a second round of financing from venturers. But for all his grumbling, he did very well. Matrix is a respected, long-established firm that operates out of Waltham, Massachusetts, a town in the high-tech belt surrounding Boston, and in Palo Alto on Sand Hill Road. In 1979, it put money behind Apple Computer, getting in about two years after Valentine and Sequoia. Sigma Partners also enjoys a high reputation. It is a neighbor to Matrix, with offices on El Camino Real in Menlo Park, and in Boston. The two firms continue to coinvest. Both backed Cascade Communications, a communications hardware company founded by entrepreneur-in-demand Gururaj "Desh" Deshpande. Cascade started as a one-man show in 1991 and grew to 900 employees by 1997, with $500 million in annual revenue. Later, Matrix became a venture funder of Deshpande's latest creation, Sycamore Networks, a maker of optical networking equipment that got off the ground in February 1998. Deshpande is in the class of superstar entrepreneurs who don't court venture capitalists; venture capitalists come calling on him.

But Ferguson gripes about his treatment by both Matrix and Sigma. Although in *High Stakes, No Prisoners* the author attests to some fights and unpleasantness with Wade Woodson, the partner at Sigma who headed up the Vermeer deal, he reserves his greatest vituperation for Andy Marcuvitz of Matrix Partners. Marcuvitz's mother must cringe at the portrait. By Ferguson's account, not only is the VC slow-witted, deceitful, self-interested, oily, and obese, he is also a very poor dresser.

The population of more than 3,500 venture capitalists practicing in the United States must include the same percentage of scoundrels as any other class of highly educated, ambitious professionals. "VCs come in all flavors, from the vultures to those who really care," observes Bard Salmon, who's seen the business from both sides. He is an inveterate entrepreneur and a new-venture investor himself, who is now president of the start-up RealityWave, which sells software that speeds the travel of complicated images over the Internet.

So, venture capitalists aren't all angels—who would argue with that? But it's also unfair and inaccurate to represent them as a class of despoilers of some sort of mythic, entrepreneurial purity.

It's hardly surprising that at Cisco, some facts surrounding the departure of Bosack and Lerner don't quite jive with the lore that's grown up around their exit. For one thing, Don Valentine says he never uttered anything about owning a desk. More importantly, new management never arrived to displace the founders. John Morgridge moved in as chief executive in 1988, two years before the 1990 departure of Bosack and Lerner. As told by Valentine, the venture capitalist who hired Morgridge, Sequoia originally backed the company with the understanding from its founders that the firm would bring in professional leadership. He says both Bosack and Lerner participated in the screening and interviewing of Morgridge. Morgridge subsequently filled out the management team with his own hires, a common practice.

Valentine describes the blowup that led to the pair's departure in 1990 as nothing more than a personality conflict. At the time, Sandy Lerner served in an executive role as customer advocate, a position the company still maintains. "One day six vice presidents came to see me," says Valentine, who was Cisco's chairman at the time. "They gave me their individual views on why either they were going to quit, or Sandy had to leave the company." When she left, Lerner took her husband, cofounder Len Bosack, with her.

Valentine's account is certainly plausible. But in the end, who cares? In the case of Cisco Systems especially, any attempt to assemble a he-said/she-said reconstruction of decade-old incidents is unnecessary and even silly, because the facts speak so clearly for themselves. Cisco has been exceedingly well managed. It not only rides the business explosion called the Internet—racking up sales record upon sales record as telecom networks stretch and swell from on-line traffic—it also helps to drive it as the preeminent supplier of switches and routers, the hardware for making network connections. Today, with 30,000 employees around the world, Cisco takes in nearly $20 billion in revenue annually. When Morgridge gave up the job of president and CEO in January 1995, his six years of leadership had brought the company from $5 million to $1.2 billion in annual sales. Morgridge still serves as chairman of the board, a role he took over from Valentine in 1995, though Valentine retains a regular board seat.

It's impossible to say what might have happened had Bosack and Lerner remained at Cisco. But a case study on the company published by Harvard Business School, prepared by Professor Richard Nolan, raises the possibility that "this early exit of the founders provided a receptive environment for laying the groundwork for disciplined management, which in turn let the company capitalize on market opportunities and grow at a phenomenal rate without derailing its focus or losing control." No matter what else you say about Don Valentine's view from the desk back in 1988, 1989, and 1990, it is deceitful to deny that he chose well when he placed John Morgridge as president and CEO.

On the other hand, by Charles Ferguson's own account in *High Stakes, No Prisoners*, it gets hard to find any decisions he made at Vermeer that didn't rear up to bite him. As much as he rails against both the deceitfulness and the inabilities of the chief executive hired to run Vermeer, Ferguson himself contributed most to the selection of John Mandile. (Mandile later became a venture capitalist with Sigma Partners.) Ferguson, among others, overruled the views of some of the company's software developers and overpriced Front-Page, scaring off buyers. He came close to derailing acquisition negotiations with Microsoft, and had to be warned off by a Microsoft executive, Chris Peters. (The detested Mandile, on the other hand, gets credit for the diplomacy that keeps the acquisition on track.)

In his own book, Ferguson comes across as suspicious and distrustful, unyielding, explosive, argumentative, and at times abusive. He also seems to be self-deluding, as when he rationalizes his own deceitfulness and manages, with some literary dexterity, to besmirch others for his lie: "So I asked myself, What would Mandile do in these circumstances? And so I decided to lie," he writes in describing a fib he told to Netscape CEO Jim Barksdale to hold off a complaint against Vermeer to the U.S. Justice Department.

Without looking very deeply between the lines, it is very easy to read *High Stakes, No Prisoners* not as a "winner's tale," as the subtitle suggests, but as the account of a start-up gone bad because the founder just wasn't cut out to run a business but was too obstinate to get out the way so others could run it. No one at Vermeer had any fun, Ferguson included. When it finally sold to Microsoft, the investors and founders and some of the key personnel made out well financially, but the acquisition comes across as a last-gasp effort by most everyone involved to get out of a situation gone sour. (Ferguson paints it as unfortunate but inevitable: Sell to Microsoft or be devoured by the giant.) Ferguson's venture investors thought the company could make an attractive public offering. His cofounder Randy Forgaard didn't want to move to Seattle or go to work for Bill Gates. Neither did some of Vermeer's most valuable, devoted software developers. But in the end, it sounds like many employees were relieved to escape Ferguson's control and join Microsoft.

When it works, the relationship between VC and entrepreneur is symbiotic. VCs need entrepreneurs. But entrepreneurs also need VCs. From the money he made on the sale of Cascade, Desh Deshpande could have started Sycamore Networks without venture dough. But the partnership he struck up with Matrix provides more than just cash. Says Bryan Stolle, "If I was to start another company, I could fund it entirely myself. But I wouldn't do that, because you want the help that those guys provide. And it's not even the help running the company, and giving advice. It's the impact of their support. The connections. The people they can get you connected to. And then the people those people can get you connected to, and so on."

Venture capital powers a machine that's tuned to get things started.

2

OTHER PEOPLE'S MONEY

Venture capitalists invest other people's money, and they have only a limited amount of time to put that money to work before they have to give it back. Those two factors discourage practitioners from behaving like the gunslinging, self-interested dilettantes they're sometimes made out to be. Sure, some may get away with it for a while, like during the heyday half-decade leading up to the year 2000, when it seemed like anybody could make a bundle by backing a company with a dotcom on its letterhead. But any venture practitioner who wants to stay in business, who wants a shot at job security approaching lifetime employment, has to please his customers.

His customers are the individuals and entities who put money into his firm's venture-capital fund. Some venture firms put some of their own assets into the pot as well. But for the most part, venture-investment funds are collected from outside investors, who entrust some of their wealth to the venture firm with the expectation that they'll get back more dollars than they originally contribute when the fund is distributed at the end of its life span. That makes for accountability: outside authorities with a keen interest in the performance of the firm and its members.

Venture funds are gathered from many corners of the capital markets. Primary contributors include university endowments, pension-plan holdings, charitable foundations, insurance companies and other financial institutions, plus wealthy families—clans with financial empires on the order of, say, the Kennedys. They're called limited partners: they enter into partnership with the venture capitalists to invest on their behalf. But as only limited partners, they don't exercise any management authority over the money. That's entrusted to the general partners alone, who are the guys who bear the distinction "venture capitalist."

A good venture firm can wear its limiteds like a badge of distinction. TA Associates, an outfit that started in 1968, lists limited partners that include endowment funds from Dartmouth, Harvard, and Notre Dame. Financial institutions like BankAmerica Capital, Metropolitan Life, and Nationwide kick into TA funds. The firm invests for the Ford Foundation, the Howard Hughes Medical Institute, the Metropolitan Museum of Art, and for pension funds from AT&T, Corning, Dow Chemical, GM, Pfizer, and from a slew of teachers' and other state and regional retirement programs. These can be long-standing relationships. Since 1978, pension programs from the states of Delaware and Michigan have ponied into the funds of Accel Partners, a Silicon Valley venture firm.

The better firms take their money carefully. "There's a strategy to raising a fund," says Jim Swartz, who has raised many for Accel, which he founded. "You want investors who are long-term, that are going to be continuous. And you want people who are high quality, who understand what you're doing, and are not just here today, gone tomorrow." That means staying away from quick-hit opportunists. Venture investments suffer vicissitudes. At times, limiteds may need to hang on and keep the faith.

In June 2000, Accel announced its latest fund, valued at $1.6 billion. That's big, but it's not unprecedented. In April 2000, Technology Crossover Ventures, a five-year-old newcomer and a neighbor to Accel in downtown Palo Alto, announced its own $1.6 billion fund, labeled TCV IV. In November 99, *Forbes* magazine gibed about how more and more venture outfits were joining the billion-buck club. Under the headline "Mine's Bigger Than Yours," the magazine listed six firms with new funds surpassing the threshold, including highfliers Benchmark Capital, Oak Investment Partners, and Redpoint Ventures.

Naturally fund size varies a lot among the 400 or so venture capital firms operating in the United States. In aggregate, they took $46 billion into new venture funds in 1999, according to Venture Economics, a research firm that follows the industry. Of course, limited partners committed all that money while demand for Internet companies still sizzled, with stock-market traders still buying up initial public offerings of young, technology companies on the Nasdaq exchange with unprecedented exuberance—bidding up stock prices to dizzying levels that paid back early investors handsomely. The exuberance looked to be fading since the Nasdaq nosedive that began in March 2000. The portent is lower future returns than limited partners grew to expect in the preceding half-decade—not losses, but not sky's-the-limit returns.

Funds also overlap. Technology Crossover closed its first fund, totaling $100 million, in June 1995, the year it set up shop. With that investment kitty still young and active, the firm raised its second, at $195 million, closing in January 1997. All told, a typical, first-line venture firm will end up investing in about forty companies per fund, with a lot of the companies getting follow-up financing in second and third rounds meant to support the budding companies after their early infusions run out.

Venture firms make their money two ways. First, firms deduct an annual management fee from their funds, usually 2.5 percent of the total. That's meant to provide the cash needed to meet regular operating expenses—all the usual business finances like salaries, supplies and equipment, office leases, travel costs, and even the occasional bottle of champagne to uncork when a company in a firm's investment portfolio pays off big. Since the management fee is a fixed percentage of the fund size, the larger the fund, the more expensive the champagne. As lucrative as a $500 million fund may be, a firm with a $1 billion kitty gets twice as much for operating expenses.

But that can work out to be chump change compared with the carry, which is the amount of earnings that venture firms retain. That can range from 20 percent to 30 percent of a fund's investment gains. Top-tier venture players typically keep 30 percent, as compensation for their consistent performance.

Limited partners are willing to give up that hefty percentage of their winnings because they expect the payback to be large enough to compensate. Being no fools, they only return to reinvest in a firm's succeeding funds if past paybacks justify it.

It's the high-growth potential of the asset class—ambitious little companies—that accounts for returns so large that limiteds willingly give up 30 percent of their investment's gains. There's no practical boundary on the upside an investor will see when a fresh young company hits it big. *If* it hits it big.

That can be a big if. Even with venture capitalists lending a hand, the odds of survival aren't the best. Figures for failure rates of venture-backed companies tend to be anecdotal, because the firms don't talk as much about their bad bets. According to Dr. Jeffrey Sohl, who directs the Center for Venture Research at the Whittemore School of Business at the University of New Hampshire, out of every ten venture-backed companies, two to four don't make it. They're dead. Another two to four are what he calls "the living dead." They survive, but they don't experience the hyper-growth necessary to significantly boost a venture firm's returns. Only one to two companies out of ten do that. Ten may be the total number of companies in a fund's investment portfolio, although it's likely to be more.

Top-tier, high-profile venture firms claim to do better. But whatever the hit rate, everyone acknowledges that new companies are tenuous entities. It's this high-risk factor, coupled with the allure of high paybacks, that accounts for venture capital's existence. VCs are needed by institutional investors who want the generous returns but who don't have the time and the resources the assets demand to attain the returns.

The setup makes venture capitalists hardworking and well-paid intermediaries between capital markets and entrepreneurs. The way the system works, the outside investors chip into a venture fund because it can pay such encouraging returns. But it takes a lot of work to earn those returns, so they turn the actual investing over to specialists—venture capitalists—who know how to identify appropriate targets, and then how to coach along the young companies to help assure their success. In a way, that makes VCs contractors working for their limited partners. And although they give the limiteds access to a lucrative asset class, the venturers also give those assets, or entrepreneurs, a conduit to capital markets that might otherwise be closed to them.

Venture capitalists specialize in developing start-up businesses. That makes them active investors—a characteristic that distinguishes them from just about every other class of money growers. It's not enough to simply toss some big sums at an ambitious new business leader, then close your eyes and trust, hope, and pray that the entrepreneur spins gold. Experience teaches that, no matter how good a business idea, the young hopefuls behind it need a lot of help to make their new company successful.

What's more, a VC has only a limited period to effect that success. That can—or should—add up to a significant constraint on a venture investor's behavior. The fund is going to be distributed at its ten-year maturity date even if the general economy is in a bust and the market for start-ups is sour.

That's a subtlety that might be lost on anyone who started in the practice within the last half-decade: Markets also turn south. In fact, venture investing is profoundly affected by the market for public companies. It even owes its good health and existence to a large, active market for public companies. Beyond the cultural values—social mobility, freedom from government interference, acceptance of technology changes as beneficial and improving—the venture system operates so vibrantly in America because the public stock markets place a sizable pot at the end of the rainbow. The logic is very simple: "It's the ability to get money out that encourages money to go in," reasons Bard Salmon, the entrepreneur and new-venture investor. His point is that not many people are going to put money into a company and then wait around for it to become the next, say, Procter & Gamble, which may take twenty-five, fifty, or one hundred years. Ebullient start-up activity may depend on a healthy venture-capital community to coax it along, but those venture capitalists depend upon a mechanism for converting their investments to tangible returns, within a reasonable time frame.

The definition of "reasonable" bounces around a bit. During the Internet-induced hysteria of the late 1990s, some new companies were spinning to a public offering in less than a year. But in a more rational environment, venture investments can take a handful of years to mature. Some may stretch out longer—to eight years, ten years—while a young company slips around trying to find its footing. That's part of the risk a VC assumes.

The primary mechanism for closing an investment is the initial public offering, when a private company first offers its equity for sale on a public stock market. Public listing gives private investors the opportunity sell their shares that hitherto had no place else to go (although the lockup provisions of an IPO prevent them from getting out fast; typically they're required to wait six months before selling shares). In the United States, the Nasdaq stock exchange makes all the difference to early-stage, private-equity investors, because its listing rules let it take smallish newcomers that don't have a long, hoary history of earnings. It offers VCs what they call an "exit strategy": the means to terminate an investment by converting their private equity to bankable returns. The other predominant exit strategy is acquisition by a big company that wants to pick up the capabilities of the venture-backed concern. The IPO is usually the preferred exit, because it has the potential to pay more.

To get a company there, venture capitalists become involved in its management, harnessing their specialized skills and services developed to address the lacks and needs of an upstart business. That doesn't mean they can salvage any wreck. Their aim is to avoid the wrecks, by carefully examining and selecting investment targets before they commit any dollars. The process is called "due diligence." It includes tasks like checking an entrepreneur's credentials; getting to know him; determining market size and potential; studying the business concept; testing it against market factors that are already known, like the positions of potential competitors; and making reasonable, informed guesses about factors unknown, such as how the new product or approach will appeal to its target customers.

Thus the investment activities of VCs divide into two broad categories. First comes the requirement to identify good companies or companies-to-be with good plans for addressing large markets. Those prospects start out with the highest probability of success. Next is the need to coach, support, nurture, and nag the companies toward their highest value possible.

It's a multistage process. The formal investment, after due diligence convinces a VC to jump, starts with a term sheet. It lays out the conditions of the agreement between the investors and the founders. The two big issues it addresses are ownership share and valuation. Those figures come as the result of negotiation, and naturally terms can vary a lot from deal to deal. Vermeer gave up 50 percent ownership to its three venture backers. Toysmart was offered a deal that would have ceded 25 percent ownership to a VC, though it gave that share to Mickey instead. For its first-in-the-door investment in Cisco, Sequoia took a third of the company, leaving a third to the half-dozen founders, with a third reserved to dole out to future employees as stock incentives to coax them to come aboard.

(One anecdote regarding early Cisco ownership has to rate as one of the biggest personal-finance gaffs of all time. Wife and husband Sandy Lerner and Len Bosack sold their Cisco shares when they left the company. At that time, Cisco was already public, completing its IPO in 1990, but the enormous run-up in its value was yet to come. It may have been an effective protest, but from the appreciation of equity that an original founder could have realized, you could send an entire high school graduating class to Harvard and still have enough left over for some very nice vacations.)

Valuation, which is the estimate of a new company's market value, determines how much a venture investor pays for his share. For new companies, setting valuation gets down to the entangling task of figuring out the worth of a small, often unknown, business that is often reliant on new and untested products that are built using new technology, often operating in a new market or even a market that's still nonexistent, and often challenging well-financed, entrenched, and frequently combative large and established companies. The negotiation can get dicey. Despite the uncertainties he faces, the entrepreneur wants a high valuation. It gives him more cash for the equity he relinquishes. On the other hand, a venture capitalist is better served by a low valuation. He'll pay less for the share he takes. Then, if the company bombs, his loss is lower. If it soars, he ends up with the same share of its market value—which is determined by percent ownership—but he paid less to get it.

Acceptance of the term sheet and a deal's final closing are only the start. Investing VCs get a board seat, which provides a launching pad for their active involvement. In addition, more financial wheedling can occur. After a first round of financing, developing start-ups typically need a second round, and often a third round, or what's called a mezzanine round, intended to carry over a company as it prepares to go public. The stakes increase at each step. Celarix, which provides software that helps companies manage shipping contracts and untangle schedules, started with a private investment of $500,000 in September 1998. In March 99, its first venture round brought it $13.5 million, followed by a second round in January 2000 for $45 million.

During follow-up financing rounds, other investors often get in the act—though venture firms may also coinvest even in the first round, spreading risk and responsibility. Agile Software started with Mohr, Davidow Ventures taking the plunge in the first round. A short six months later, Sequoia Capital entered during the second round. Accel Partners bought in at third-round financing—all told, an impressive trio.

Along with venture firms, other private investors may also buy in. When venture pros Benchmark Partners and Greylock coinvested in Red Hat Software in September 98, they were joined by Intel and Netscape. Six months after that tranche, Compaq, IBM, Novell, and Oracle joined the family with minority equity investments. Before Boo.com derailed, it attracted coinvestors from well outside the venture fold, including the investment bank Goldman Sachs, and Luciano Benetton, head of the family that runs the hip clothing chain.

These basic operating practices get scrambled into all sorts of variations by the hundreds of firms practicing venture capital. One standout is In-Q-Tel, which fills its own category. Actually, In-Q-Tel is a 501c3 not-for-profit corporation. It is fully funded by the CIA, but claims the only influence on its investment decisions are the technology needs of the agency. In-Q-Tel was set up to serve as an independent bridge between the CIA and entrepreneurs who "are not interested in dealing with government bureaucracy and paper work," says Chris Tucker, chief strategist who works out of Q's Arlington, Virginia, office. It digs deeply into the spy agency's technology needs, looks for entrepreneurs who may fill them, and then helps the entreps develop the technology. It made five equity investments in its first year, 1999, and by the middle of 2000 it was approaching a few liquidity events—the cash-out, when private shares are converted to liquid assets that count as an investment return.

But Q is more an anomaly than a variation. Other firms operate closer to the model. Fidelity Ventures runs like a conventional venture investor, but doesn't raise funds outside of its family. Instead, it relies on its parent, Fidelity Investments, for capital to infuse into upstart businesses. That affects accountability: Instead of answering to a collection of limited partners, Fidelity's venture arm has to please only the bean counters of its own parent company, who share office space in the same building in Boston's financial district. Rather than drawing from a pool, Fidelity VCs must get approval from corporate bosses for each buy-in. Earnings are retained by the parent. So although the arrangement may liberate the operation from fund-raising, it submits it to over-the-shoulder scrutiny by financial professionals who don't necessarily understand the idiosyncrasies of new-venture investing.

Technology Crossover Ventures invests from a fund it hustles up like any other conventional firm, from limited partners that include General Motors, the MacArthur Foundation, Hewlett Packard, BankBoston, and Nationwide Insurance. However, it is chartered to invest not just in private companies, but also in young public concerns that are still in their high-growth stage. It does that through a separate fund, called the TCV Franchise Fund, which was still being built as of early 2000.

Some firms go after a particular segment of the private-equity field. TA Associates hunts for small, youngish companies that have nevertheless been around long enough to establish themselves. They're entrepreneurial concerns still, but they're typically already selling a product or service that's yielding some revenue. Most have bootstrapped themselves, making TA the first institutional investor in the door. "The people that we're backing have successfully proven themselves to a point, and therefore we have that to look at. We have customers to talk to, and we know there's a market," explains Jacqueline Morby, VC and a managing director of TA, which has offices in Silicon Valley, Boston, and Pittsburgh. That slants preinvestment due diligence away from some of the intelligent guesswork that can characterize work with raw start-ups. "When you do very early stage companies, you can go through several iterations of the product, and figuring out the market, and taking different approaches to sales and marketing until you finally come up with something that works," she says. "When you invest in a company that's already done that part, you may pay a higher price to get in, but it's quicker to get it to be successful."

Nevertheless, from-scratch companies can more often provide the most spectacular returns. Therefore many venture firms specialize as early-stage investors that back very young companies and even pre-companies, which may be nothing more than a founder or two promoting what looks like it may turn into a good idea. The firms may operate incubators, where they give these young hopefuls office space, advice, and a lot of encouragement to develop the idea. Incubation may even entail building a company from scratch from an idea a VC conceived on his own, rather than one that walked in with a would-be entrepreneur. Early-stage investors tend to get the most public attention—and even, at times, adulation—because their successes can be so spectacular. They also tend to characterize the popular image of venture capital, because of the greater risk involved, and the frenetic work pace required to stave off failure.

But for all the hoopla they attract, first-round venturers aren't quite the biggest risk-takers in new-business funding. Typically, seed funding—the smallest, riskiest investments, because the business is just a tenuous, very early-stage concept—comes from angel investors. They're a special class of venturer, separate from organized, institutional venture capital. Angels are individuals investing their own money. In a way, they're disorganized venture capital.

A starting, angel round of financing for an entrepreneur is a lot smaller than a later, venture deal. Typically, angel infusions tally in the hundreds of thousands of dollars, rather than the millions that institutional venture capitalists kick in.

"This is my money, and there's a lot less of it," quips Jim Hynes, who became an angel when he retired young as head of Fidelity Ventures at the end of 99. "I'm a little more conservative, and I'm a little more protective. I really have to like something to jump, because I don't have as much money to diversify myself around," he says, which is the way an organized venture firm spreads its risk with positions in many companies.

Bard Salmon, the RealityWave chairman, was one of fifteen angels who helped the company Starnex get its start in providing Internet software to insurance brokers. Later, venture capitalists came in with a financing round that brought $10 million. Now Salmon sits on the board along with two VCs. "How do we operate differently? They do it full-time and we just do it part-time. They have a partnership structure and we're private. And they have a big fund but we have a small wallet," says Salmon. Otherwise, he sees himself coaching the entrepreneur and contributing expertise to the company the same as the professional venture players.

Salmon is a big-business veteran, having toiled for Bethlehem Steel, Honeywell, and Computervision, once a software-industry star. But since he abandoned the corporate establishment fifteen years ago, he's been involved in about a dozen start-ups, as either funder or entrepreneur. He backs small businesses today almost for the sport.

"I love it, and that is far stronger than the financial opportunity," he explains. "In fact, it is rather illiquid. Once you're in, you're stuck, and it can take a very long time. Even when you think in the beginning it will be short, it can take ten years. You have to have high tolerance for risk, and to huge fluctuations from an emotional standpoint. In fact, you have to almost thrive on those things. But if you're doing it just for the money, you're going to fail."

Venture capitalists do it for the money. It's the payoff, after all, that brings big investors into their funds. But the better VCs also play for sheer love of the undertaking.

"The companies that I'm most proud of are the ones that almost didn't make it," says William Kaiser, who has practiced venture capital for Greylock since 1986. "They're not necessarily the ones that were the biggest wins, or that gave the greatest returns to Greylock. They're the ones that faced incredible adversity, including, in some cases, near death, and managed to recover."

3

THE MONEY SALESMAN

Rick Burnes reduces the practice of venture capital to a single sound bite: "We're money salesmen."

Really?

"We try to get capable entrepreneurs to take our money, and rather than getting an interest rate, we own a piece of their company."

Of course, as the long-ago founder of Charles River Ventures, Richard M. Burnes knows better than anyone that his simplification leaves out a lot of vital detail. And as a thoughtful and consistently successful venture capitalist, he understands he can either fill a volume with the lessons culled from his experiences or he can very cleverly reduce them all to a unifying principle.

"Venture capital is nothing but good judgment: having reasonable information and exercising good judgment. That sounds very easy. It's not very profound. Of course, coming in out of the rain is not very exciting either, but you don't get wet." He laughs.

Burnes can't suppress the fun-loving and playful side of his nature. It even shows up at www.crv.com, Charles River's Web site. Its homepage recently showed a team photo of the general partners arrayed beaming in their shirtsleeves around a conference table that had been carried out into the snow. The site includes a whole room titled Fun Stuff, with a lengthy glossary explaining the terms of Venture Speak. It's intended as a good-natured, chiding spoof of the idiosyncrasies of venture capital, and maybe also as a whimsical admonishment against pompous behavior. The section called A Guide to What Venture Capitalists Say reveals that when a VC labels someone an "independent thinker," the English translation makes him a "complete crackpot." An episode described by a VC as a "learning experience" translates to "sheer hell," and when one tells you, "thanks for your input," he means, "I'm going to completely ignore your advice." The Engineer's Dictionary—after all, as a specialty investor in technology companies, Charles River associates with a lot of engineers—tells the technically oriented that when a marketing person says, "Preliminary results are inconclusive," what he means in engineer's language is, "It blew up." When, to the marketer, "modifications are underway to correct certain problems," an engineer would simply say, "It blew up again."

The Fun Stuff room also links to the Web site www.TheVC.com. Subtitled The Surreal World of Silicon Valley Venture Capital, the site is a collection of comic strips by Robert von Goeben, a venture capitalist himself, and Kathryn Siegler, an artist and designer. Similar in spirit to the Charles River glossaries, the strips chide venture practitioners for shortcomings like inflated egos, callousness, self-importance, and shortsightedness. The cartoon labeled "The VC 19.0; The Visit to Sand Hill Road" depicts two callow, hopeful techno-geeks who are out seeking funding on the venture circuit. They're wearing Converse All-Stars sneakers and feeling awed by a venture firm's offices. When they get preoccupied by the squeaks of their soles on the marble floor, the waiting VC interrupts them: "At $7.50 a square foot, we can't afford to have a sense of humor. Let's get started."

Clearly this is inside humor. Since the comic strips are written as parodies specifically of Silicon Valley ventures, you have to wonder if by connecting to them, Charles River is less concerned with self-censorship and more intent on taking a swipe at its west coast cousins. After all, under Burnes's leadership, Charles River retains an Atlantic Coast orientation. "We're Bostonians," he declares. "It's hard to measure this, but over the last 10 years there are only a couple of firms doing as well out in Palo Alto as we are here. There's plenty to do here. There's plenty to do there." Yet even there, in Silicon Valley, new-economy capitalists grin at The VC comic strips. On TheVC.com's own homepage, J. Neil Weintraub pronounces the comics "hilarious, a must read for Silicon Valley." Weintraub's 21st Century Internet Venture Partners, though head-quartered in San Francisco, keeps a second office suite in the Valley well occupied. The firm plays in the heart of the dotcom frenzy.

But no matter how much he enjoys whimsy and laughter, there can be no question that Rick Burnes takes venture capital very seriously. He cofounded Charles River Ventures in 1970, and as managing partner he has built it into one of the most consistently successful firms in the industry. He worries out loud about the state and the direction of venture capital and the high-tech innovators it supports. At the Red Herring's Venture Market East conference in Boston in September 1999, he lamented that greed and get-rich-quick stratagems were filling in for traditional new-venture goals, like building a sustainable business that's solidly organized around competent people. Burnes cares about venture capital and the changes reshaping it.

So when he quips that venture capitalists are money salesmen, he doesn't intend to demean his profession. He means that venture capital operates in a market. Specifically, it operates in the competitive market for high-growth companies. That's the business at its most fundamental level, when you strip away all the mystique and the good and the bad images people draw and the suspicions of alchemy that arise when suddenly society notices that a small set of its brethren appears to be doing very well for itself. Although historically it's had its ups and downs, since about 1995 venture capital has done so well for itself that people couldn't miss its success. It also grew more conspicuous on account of the Internet. As that newfangled communication method rose so quickly to such lofty prominence, people noticed that alongside it stood these guys called venture capitalists who were somewhat, somehow, and in some way responsible for it. "In the last five years venture capital has gotten so much attention," says Burnes. "We all labored in the vineyards of obscurity for so long, which is just what we like, and no one knew what we were doing, and we did perfectly well. But the extremes of success have really brought the spotlights on us. It's just a fact."

The fact is that venture capital has grown up. It's no longer a cottage industry populated exclusively by craftsmen working outside of the investment mainstream. Sure, it remains a separate and distinct branch of finance, but by now it has grown both widely recognized and well situated as the cultivator of high-growth new businesses. It has established entrepreneurialism as an element of the cultural ethos, providing a dependable source for its raw material. It has lured more professionals into the practice. It has grown more competitive. It has attracted greater public scrutiny. Amid these changes, a lot of venture capitalists are exploring new investment approaches and different organizational structures in order to consolidate their gains and secure their positions against future uncertainties. After all, no one in the industry with any sense of history expects it to escape boom-and-bust business cycles.

Therefore, at the same time, experienced VCs are taking care to preserve many of the tradesmen-like practices of their profession, to assure their success even when the venture market turns hostile—or at least when it demands more than the blind bets on dotcoms that seemed to be the only requirements for success in venture capital in 1998 and 99.

Venture capital works according to the same mechanisms that determine the dynamics of any market. A market is simply a place of exchange, where people get together to trade what one side has for what the other wants. Free markets—which work according to what's called free-market economics—operate without meddling by powerful elites, which might be governments or dictators or even just the cronies who run a place. In free markets, participants aren't restricted in their deal-making. There is basic civil law to enforce contracts and such, but there aren't a whole lot of regulations stipulating what people must buy or sell, or how much or how little they must pay, or who they must bargain with, and so on. They're free to make their own decisions.

In the United States, venture capital operates largely in a free market. Participants can't get away with fraud, but beyond decent civil behavior, they don't have a lot of oversight that says they have to select this type of company, for instance, or favor that type of technology. In terms of what to buy and how much to pay, they're pretty much left to their wiles. Venture capital is also an open market, which means it is free from overbearing restrictions on who can join, and there is no limit on how many people can enter the field. Dr. Jeffrey Sohl, the director of the Center for Venture Research, considers the unrestricted freedom of the venture business one of its considerable strengths. Investors make selections based only on their estimation of a company's eventual worth. Its worth—how much people are willing to pay for it—will depend on the value of the goods or services it provides. A company that makes something that a lot of people want has a higher worth because investors expect it to return more to them as a consequence of the prosperity it will enjoy. That simple formula skews new-company selection toward the upstarts most likely to make a contribution by producing coveted products, that is, products that somehow serve people.

That's all just elementary economics. But it's worth reviewing because in a lot of quarters the free operation of a market isn't considered so constructive. By the late 1990s, probably because so much money was being made so conspicuously in some exchange places like the stock market and the venture market, the idea of free markets began drawing a lot of fire from some prominent social critics. No less a personage than the staffed and mitered Pope John Paul II came out and called them something just shy of evil, because they fail to address compassionate concerns, like caring for the poor.

The counterpoint to that view is the idea that, with a few exceptions like the infirm who legitimately need looking after, people do best when they're at liberty to care for themselves. That argument depends on a clear understanding of liberty, which here means two things. It means economic liberty, which is the freedom to use your property to your own advantage. It also means individual political liberty, which prevents ruling elites from jiggering markets to work for them. In earlier times, like the age in which Tom Jefferson wrote that "all Men are created equal," ruling elites were called the aristocracy. Later, about the time George Orwell wrote, "some animals are more equal than others," the ruling elites he had in mind were more likely to be called the Party. But they operate the same despite the name change. For markets to work well, everyone has to have the same fair shot at making their own decisions.

After that, the argument for free markets for all rests on the assumption that people are intelligent enough to seize opportunities. In a free and open market that is guarded by civil law, opportunities arise indiscriminately, to every person present. They're unpredictable, and they vary in magnitude, but chances to do well always come up.

At the farmers' market you'll buy strawberries from a grower selling them at seventy-five cents per quart rather than from a stall farther down where they're priced one dollar per quart. If enough shoppers make the same decision, the berry grower at a dollar-per either has to cut his prices or cart a lot of unsold berries back to his barn to rot. If he goes all the way down to seventy cents per quart, then the seventy-five-cent grower will have to reduce his prices, too, or he'll be the farmer who ends up with the unsold fruit. This little contest will make the farmers very anxious, but the berry shoppers will benefit. Since they're able to buy more berries for their money, they may even buy out both berry growers, sending each back to the ranch with dungarees stuffed with cash (though less cash than the fruitmen had originally hoped for), while the shoppers return to their own homes carrying a greater bounty of berries than they ever imagined.

On the other hand, if one farmer happens to be the son-in-law of the man who runs the market, or maybe if he even just buys the market owner a nice lunch, he might persuade the market chief to ban other berry growers. After that there's nothing to prevent the son-in-law from going back up to a buck per quart. He might even double his original price, demanding two dollars per quart. He'll sell a lot fewer berries that way, but he'll still make out just fine, since he'll get more money for each of the few strawberries he sells. On the other hand, far fewer people will eat strawberries, and those who do will be poorer for their purchase.

A lot of other factors influence the behaviors that govern markets. For example, if shoppers have a lot of money to spend, and if they really want strawberries, they'll keep buying them even as prices drift upward. Or if a blight wipes out most berry crops, a surviving grower can raise his prices. Some people won't be able to afford his fruits, but he won't have enough for everybody, anyway.

The market dynamics of venture capital grew very extreme at the tail end of the twentieth century. The outside attention that Rick Burnes laments was both a cause and a consequence of a gluttonous inrush of money to buy up new companies. As VCs funded the Internet, and as the Internet grew by leaps and bounds, venture successes grew conspicuous. To get in on the winnings, limited partners ceded larger and larger sums to venture funds. With more money to invest, venture capitalists stoked entrepreneurial activity even more, inflaming technology creation and the company building that occurs alongside it. With so much investment money chasing after entrepreneurs, venture capital became a sellers' market: Company creators could command higher prices for the equity that VCs expect them to give up.

In fact, Edward Kane speculates that the Internet owes much of its breathless arrival and its lightning-fast buildup to the ready availability of venture capital to fund the exploration of the countless new ideas that cumulatively account for it. By comparison, earlier technological revolutions like semiconductors were capital constrained. New ways to use microprocessors and other semiconductor products might have arrived sooner than they did, in faster succession, if more venture money had been around then, says Kane, who is senior managing director of Harborvest Partners, a Boston-based venture capital and money management firm he started in 1979. In terms of the sheer science involved, "the technological breakthrough of the semiconductor dwarfs the Internet," he says. But the Internet has boosted the fortunes of venture capital far more than semiconductor development did.

The Internet is one of several circumstances that contributed greatly to venture capital's stunning successes of the late 1990s. It provided what's called the opportunity set: a large new territory to be built up, providing a receptive business arena in which entrepreneurs can perform blank-slate innovations.

A rich opportunity set is like having a big open field to run around in. The swings and the slide and the rest of the playground equipment hasn't yet filled up with other kids. In fact, there isn't even any playground equipment in place yet. There are no weighty precedents to be overcome. There are no accepted ideas that say you have to do things this way. There are no domineering, mammoth corporations ready to squash innovation in order to keep upstarts from treading on their turf.

"If there are no good growth ideas for entrepreneurs to work on, then I suppose that will reduce returns," says Henry McCance, the managing general partner at Greylock, speaking with characteristic diffidence. McCance possesses a sense of surety about his profession that could only come after more than thirty years of successful venturing. He is a dean among venture capitalists. But nothing in the demeanor of Henry McCance expresses arrogance or boastfulness or even overweaning pride. He is justly proud, to be sure. Spare and tightly built, he can't suppress his satisfaction as he walks a visitor through the hallways of Greylock's subtly energized offices in a high-rise in Boston's financial district, stopping to detail circumstances about this and that particular company whose prospectus hangs as part of the long gallery of Greylock investments gone public. He beams that there are others, but that the firm has run out of wall space to display them. He conveys a sense of humility, and gratitude for his association with his trade. He exudes a sincerity that makes it impossible to doubt the deep conviction of his views on venture capital.

"It's not a phenomenon that I focus on very much," he continues, "because I believe that the number of good entrepreneurial growth ideas in technology and the pace and change of technology has given venture capitalists plenty to work with throughout my career in the business. I've never been sitting around saying there's no good ideas. It was a fun time to be in this business in the late 70s and early 80s, when the personal computer came out on the scene. It was a fun time to be in this business in the days when biotechnology first became involved. It's pretty heavy stuff, and I truly believe that biotechnology has a major part in revolutionizing the development of therapeutics, and a tremendous opportunity to improve the quality of life and healthcare in very exciting ways in the next 30 to 50 years. It hasn't run its course at all. But neither of those exciting events were half as important, in my opinion, or half as large, or anywhere near as big as the current changes that are being made possible by the Internet and online computing and all of its close relatives."

If there is one thing that VCs agree on, it is that the Internet represents an opportunity set so large that it will keep paying for a while to come—despite the inevitable missteps and blunders and cooldowns in the hype and even the stock market's return to sanity. "If the Internet to you means consumer-dot-com, then, yeah, you're in big trouble," echoes Jim Swartz, who is founder of Accel Partners in Palo Alto and a VC with only a few years less tenure than McCance. "To us, the Internet is more about infrastructure. It's software that enables people to run their businesses. We can keep on doing that kind of stuff for a long time."

Web technology not only represents the kind of historical discontinuity that can keep business creation humming for a while to come. It also is largely a software-based industry—although it encompasses some significant hardware opportunities as well, particularly for network equipment from people like Cisco and Sycamore, which telecommunications companies buy eagerly to keep up with demands from the everexpanding population of Internet users. But beyond telecommunications infrastructure, the I-way runs on a lot of software, and software is simply more inviting and accommodating for new business starts. It doesn't demand expensive manufacturing equipment, or prolonged engineering cycles, or the coordination of as many diverse corporate operations required to make a physical product, like a car or a computer. "The ease and low cost of going into the soft businesses has to do with their soft assets," observes Bard Salmon the entrepreneur plus angel investor. "They're cheap, and so it's much easier to get in."

For the most part, Internet business isn't about creating new technology. It's about dreaming up innovative and profitable ways to use the technology that's now established. That opens entrepreneurialism not just to independently minded wizards in white lab coats, but also to bright kids with a knack for reassembling ideas in ways that win buyers.

"We've shifted from a technology emphasis to a marketing emphasis, and that's particularly true with the Internet," says Burnes, who is another VC who would make anybody's list of seasoned veterans. "When the venture capital world focused on technical entrepreneurs, we were dealing with a very, very narrow slice of the potential managers in the country. Whereas today, 90 percent of the kids who are graduating from business school have the potential to start an Internet business. One of the reasons why we're going through this boom period is the Internet's emphasis on marketing as opposed to technology. For all intents and purposes the technology is not a factor. The key is understanding how to serve a customer. Or even how to figure out how to serve a customer."

It also helps that entrepreneurial zeal has grown so infectious that company creation is now a bona fide career path. "So many more people want to be entrepreneurs than ever did before," observes Jacqueline Morby, who has seen a lot of them come and go in her nearly twenty-five years at TA Associates. "They can see all the visible successes. They want to do that too. They are very bright people, and they're starting to get trained earlier. Now, you can't give somebody in college all the experience that a business person goes through. But you certainly can give them a good start."

For example, Stanford University runs the Technology Ventures Program, which aims to teach science and technology majors about the principles of starting and running a business. Students get to hear lectures by the likes of Kleiner-Perkins VC John Doerr, and Netscape founder Marc Andreessen. They attend classes on strategy, international expansion issues, and even gritty, get-started fundamentals like how to write a compelling business plan. Assistant director Tina Seelig says the program is so popular it must turn away about two-thirds of the students who want to get in. "Entrepreneurship is part of the spirit of our community here," she says. "It obviously got revved up with the whole Internet and Web revolution, but people have been very entrepreneurial in the Bay Area for decades." Stanford is in Palo Alto, on the Silicon Valley side of San Francisco Bay.

All told, when you take the expansive opportunity set called the Internet, combine it with the fact that its opportunities are fundamentally easier to exploit, and add to that the fact that more people than ever before are eager to exploit them, it amounts to a lot of raw material for venture capital, all of it appearing from about 1995 onward. At the same time, the stock market's late enthusiasm for young technology companies also contributed an awful lot to the priming of the venture profession. By the summer of 2000 it was widely acknowledged that the bidding up of stock prices that started roughly at the kick-off of the holiday season in November 1998, and ended in March 2000, was a legitimate bubble—an irrational stock-buying binge that threw sound business judgment out the window. In a July 14, 2000, postmortem, the *Wall Street Journal* declared that the craze "ranks among history's biggest bubbles. Investment bankers, venture capitalists, research analysts and investors big and small, through cynicism or suspension of disbelief, financed and took public countless companies that had barely a prayer of prospering. Rarely have so many people willingly put prudence on hold to enter a game most were sure wouldn't last"

Like all irrational mass movements, it's tough to say exactly what caused this one—other than irrationality. But it's clear that the allure of the Internet bore at least some of the responsibility for the insanely high valuations public investors attached to new technology companies. "In the extraordinary enthusiasm for this new platform, the Internet, investor enthusiasm got ahead of reality," speculates John Fisher of Draper Fisher Jurvetson. "It still represents the biggest business opportunity ever. It's just that it's going to take several decades to play out."

As it does, the equity markets will still welcome new companies that can demonstrate some legitimate value, or at least a strong potential to deliver value. "There always will be a market for good companies, even in the worst of times," assures Jacqui Morby with the perspective earned through more than two decades in the practice. Still, no one expects the stock-buying frenzy to resume any time soon. "I don't think we'll ever see again what we saw over the course of the last 24 months," said Fisher in May 2000. "Not in our lifetimes. It may happen again sometime toward the second half of this new century, but I don't think I'll ever see it again."

But its effects are already etched into the venture business. Much of the late-boom money that flushed into venture capital funds became trapped in pre-IPO investments that lost much chance of ever paying the extreme returns people came to expect from the few years when Internet starts couldn't lose. What's worse, the investments were made at very high valuations, which is what the equity sellers' market of the late 1990s demanded. As a consequence, experienced VCs expect fund returns to decline. This is where market economics takes over.

When so much money rushes into the system that venture capitalists have to all but beg entrepreneurs to take it, which drives up the prices the VCs pay for their equity stakes, venture returns eventually decline. It's simply harder to get a high return on equity when you've paid too much for that equity. Think of it as the venture variation of buying high and selling low, which is not a good formula for success in any investment arena. Reacting to the lower returns, limited partners cut back on the sums they dole into venture funds. Therefore, venture money becomes more dear. With their supply of capital constrained, entrepreneurs have to work harder to get it. The environment shifts from a sellers' market, favoring the business starters with equity to sell, to a buyers' market, favoring the venture funders looking to purchase growth-company equity. The venture capitalists who stay in the game can then pay lower prices, or valuations, to get the ownership shares they seek. In that climate, when an investment's worth increases, the venture returns are higher, because the VCs spent less to acquire the equity. They're buying low, selling high.

Of course, as venture returns start to swell again and limited partners take note, they'll grow generous once more with their contributions to venture funds. As money floods into the venture system, and valuations rise, the cycle turns and starts to repeat.

Henry McCance has witnessed such loops before. By his lights, the upswing phase of the investment cycle is what played out through the 1990s. The supply of new-venture capital constricted after a period of relatively low returns in the middle to late 80s. That made it harder for entrepreneurs to find finance, putting VCs in command of valuations with a buyers market. Therefore coming into the 1990s they were purchasing small-company equity for relatively low prices. Serendipitously, the Internet arrived, expanding opportunities. With it came a nine- to ten-year bull run in the public markets, culminating with the stock-market frenzy that significantly increased the exit values VCs got for their investments. "In the last 15 years, the planets could not have been better aligned for spectacular venture results. And indeed the industry's results have been spectacular," says McCance.

But the planets' spin became tough to divine by the turn of the century. Still, according to market patterns, a run of lower returns appeared to await venture investors. Experienced venture investors knew enough to await it.

Observed Jacqui Morby: "the problem for the whole industry is going to be, when this public market goes away, and all the valuations go down again, we will have paid valuations up here, but our exit multiples will be way down here. So there will be a slump in ROIs for all venture capital programs like there was in the middle '80s." She laid out that scenario in early 2000, right about the time the public market was in fact going away.

But that doesn't mean that venture capital will return to the spot where it stood in 1990 or even 1995. It's seen too many far-reaching changes. The field has grown larger. Its cultural and commercial impact has grown in significance. The surrounding world has noticed that fact. The ineluctable progression of technology, its playground, has led to new capabilities and even new rules for businesses that themselves affect the way venturers must operate.

"The venture business right now is very different than it was historically," states Seth Neiman. "Everybody and their dog is a venture capitalist," he adds as a plaintive lament. Neiman himself, who practices at Silicon Valley's Crosspoint Venture Partners, joined the profession only in the middle 90s. But compared with many, he already displays the aspect of a gritty veteran.

The count of practicing VCs swelled to 3,658 in 2000, from about 2,883 just three years earlier, according to the 2000 National Venture Capital Yearbook, prepared by Venture Economics. A slumping industry with a smaller investment cache simply won't need all the manpower, and therefore it's likely that some of the young bloods who entered the trade in its late 90s heyday will flush out. But not all of them will exit. Short tenure by itself doesn't make a venture capitalist incapable or undetermined.

Before Michael Linnert came to Silicon Valley in 1994, he wasn't even exactly sure where the place lay. Somewhere or other out west, he shrugged. He had earned a bachelor's in electrical engineering from Notre Dame. Then he had passed a year as a manufacturing engineer at a GM shock-absorber plant before traveling to New York to work in the financial institutions group for investment bankers Goldman Sachs. It was Goldman that introduced him to the Valley, transferring Linnert to its technology group there. He cut out to earn his MBA at Stanford, and then, still professionally wandering and ever inquisitive, Linnert worked briefly as a product manager at 3Com, the Silicon Valley producer of communications and computer networking products. Until some former associates from his Goldman days introduced him to Palo Alto's Technology Crossover Ventures in 1997, Linnert had been blissfully, naively unaware of exactly how VCs operated. Today he is still only a start-up venture capitalist, graduating to general partner at the firm in 1999. But he feels little uncertainty about his position. "The fundamental opportunities of the Internet to create huge businesses aren't going to go away over the next ten years," he estimates. "That's ten years of fundamental change in which I'll have a job. I'm comfortable with that. I think there'll be plenty of work for us all to do."

Athletically lank, youthful, fair-skinned, and a tad on the ruddy side, Linnert is emblematic of the new VCs. His firm, Technology Crossover, is composed largely of latecomers. It opened shop only in 1995, when founders Jay Hoag and Rick Kimball spied opportunities in Internet-ventures investing. That was the era in which rustling up limited partners to stuff venture funds was relatively easy. As recently as early April 2000, the firm closed its TCV IV fund at $1.6 billion, a tally that makes it the largest ever venture fund devoted exclusively to Internet growth companies, according to the firm's claims. As the fund size shows, Technology Crossover is ambitious and determined. It considers itself a long-haul player. And it has as good a shot at survival and prosperity as anybody, including the long-established firms. After all, venture capital isn't immune from changes and challenges. Just as it foments rebellion and reshuffling in other industries, venture investing can undergo reorganization as aggressive upstarts with better ideas sneak up on the status quo.

"There's no divine right here," asserts Jake Reynolds, Linnert's colleague and a general partner at Technology Crossover Ventures. "The people who jumped on the Internet and took advantage of it and invested heavily in it have reaped the benefits. And others who were slow and who were not believers allowed folks like us to exist. I mean, there would not be a need for TCV if the Internet had been a strong focus of all the blue-chip venture capital firms that were in existence five years ago. Basically, you've got to perform. And you've got to be in the right place at the right time. And you've got to pick where the world is moving, or you're going to get left behind."

That risk confronts both camps, the seasoned vets and the ambitious tyros, especially if dwindling returns force a significant slowdown in the investments limited partners place in venture funds. VCs have complained for at least a half-decade about how energetically they must compete to close deals with first-class entrepreneurs, on account of all the other VCs eager to snare the same deals. They could suddenly find themselves competing for a share of dwindling fund money, as well.

At the same time, technology changes are writing new rules for all parties. "The Internet enables companies to grow faster than they have been able to grow in the past," observes John Fisher. "This extraordinary platform right now connects 400 million people on the planet [as of early 2000], and some day it will probably connect 70 percent of the population of the planet. Call it four or five billion people. As a result of those connections, businesses can offer their wares and their services at speeds that were never before attainable. They can grow very fast. This is a new distribution paradigm." That fact may justify the high stock-market valuations for some new-economy companies that critics call ridiculously high. Even after the March 2000, precipitous drop in share prices, some Internet-company equities continued to sell at prices that gave the outfits market capitalizations many times their revenues, never mind their profits. But Fisher's point is that right now, amid the creative hubbub, it's not possible to say how high is too high. That's the point about a paradigm shift: It's a change of the accepted rules. "Everybody is trying to figure it out. The Street is trying to figure it out. The analysts are trying to figure it out, and the open market is doing what it's doing," says the VC.

"The pace of change is accelerating everywhere," concurs Jacqui Morby. That's another consequence of the Internet. The near-instant spread of information through electronic media can change the rules about competitive advantage. It's tough to claim any to-day. Morby tells how even Pacific Life, a Fortune 500 insurance company where she serves on the board of directors, finds competi-tors matching its new products almost as soon as they're released. "It used to be five or six months before their competitors even knew what they were selling that was doing so well. Now they have competition in a month," she explains.

And that's the insurance industry. In the high-tech fields where venture capitalists play, the loss of first-out-the-door, proprietary advantage can be crippling.

Whether the changes they face are cyclical or secular and perma-nent, many venture firms have been moving amid the simmering uncertainty to fortify their positions and, they hope, sustain their prosperity into the future. Venture capital itself is rife with innova-tion and experimentation as many of its adherents search for modi-fied business models that might trump the traditional practices.

Draper Fisher Jurvetson is one leader of the innovation, if only for the size of its ambitions and the number of programs it is trying. In one, it has created a franchise of venture practices spread across the United States and even reaching overseas. The separate opera-tions in Boston, Chicago, Denver, Los Angeles, New York, Pitts-burgh, Portland, Salt Lake City, and Seattle were set up as affiliate funds between 1998 and 2000. Each is separately managed, with separate general partners, and with its own investment pool, or fund, to which Draper Fisher Jurvetson contributes. The idea is for each to invest in early-stage start-ups within its region. Critics, mostly competing VCs, call it McVenture-Capital: cloning the Draper Fisher Jurvetson name in order to get in on more deals, but thereby diluting its reputation. John Fisher says the program aims to create a network effect, which will make the affiliates better in-vestors by giving them access to the widespread, global resources of the DFJ family. It's a variation on the argument that the whole is greater than the sum of the parts.

In another curious turn, in the summer of 2000, the firm launched its VC Draper Fisher Jurvetson Fund I. It's set up as a closed-end mutual fund. A fixed number of shares are available to ordinary investors, to let them own a piece of venture capital.

Battery Ventures is modifying the traditional organizational structure of a firm in an effort to make more consistent and effective investments. "Many firms are a loose collection of maybe half a dozen gunslinger partners. Maybe each one of them has a secretary, but that's about it," states Battery general partner Oliver Curme. "When they pull the trigger on a deal they come back and they get some kind of approval at the partnership meeting. But the partnership is only a loose coalition of independent guys who provide some measure of risk reduction. So if you're a biotech guy and you have three lean years, you're not going to go out of business because the communications or the software guys will carry you, and vice versa."

On the other hand, of Battery's 30 investment professionals, only eleven are investing partners. The other nineteen are what the firm calls principals, plus senior associates, associates, and analysts underneath them. The analysts are on the front line, taking inquiries from entrepreneurs. When they find one that looks appealing, says Curme, "we put together a team of three, sometimes four people to work on the deal together. The junior people have lots of time, but not the experience. The senior people have lots of experience, but not the time. The senior partner can provide the guidance to the team, and move things along."

But the teams don't only work on specific deals. They also form around project areas: hot fields thought to hold promise for start-up businesses. "They'll be researching an area on and off for a year or eighteen months sometimes before they identify the right investment opportunity. Sometimes we'll look in an area and we'll look and we'll look and we won't find a company that fits our investment profile. So we go off and create it," says Curme. "It's an organizational approach, opposed to this gunslinger approach, and I'm optimistic that it can scale. The prevailing, accepted wisdom in the venture business is that it has no economies of scale. You can't really scale well. You're limited to a loose collection of gunslingers.

But I think there's a chance that this industry is going to go through a big change from a bunch of little boutiques to being consolidated into a few dominant organizations that really drive the industry."

Still, other firms in dominant positions feel they can lead the industry by adhering resolutely to the time-tested practices that made them. Greylock, for one, gives equal time even to its portfolio companies that aren't shaping up to be the billion-dollar winners that boost a firm's returns. And its partners have a reputation for staying longer on a company's board of directors, remaining even post-IPO, to help keep the company pointed in a profitable direction. Its motive is to demonstrate to new-business starters that Greylock is entrepreneur friendly, and not just interested in turning a quick buck.

"A big key to great results," says battle-hardened Henry Mc-Cance, "is to make sure first of all that your firm has such a reputation of excellence that the best entrepreneurs knock on your door and give you a chance to sell. And then, when you get that shot, that you win more than your fair share of the competitive deals. By not abandoning the company that is going through trouble, we are earning our reputation. And in this industry, reputation is everything. Hard to earn. Hard to keep. Easy to lose."

Underlying his confidence is a boundless enthusiasm for venture itself. "Long term it's still a great industry," declares McCance. "It's a great industry for one simple reason. It's that small companies can grow faster, can innovate quicker, are not hindered by legacy, bureaucratic thinking, so they can take advantage of new technology quicker, and, most of all, if you have a little luck—and luck is a big part in this business—and if you execute well, and you're in the right marketplaces, you can create compound growth rates in companies that IBM can't possibly do, or that AT&T can't possibly do. It's just simply easier to compound at one hundred percent a year when you've got a one million or a ten million revenue base, than when you've got a ten billion base."

4

THE PERSONALITY FACTOR

Venture capitalists recite with stunning unanimity that the single most important ingredient to a successful start-up is the people who run it. That makes their job sound easy enough. Want a successful investment? You simply have to discover or assemble a capable, high-quality management team. But finding good business leaders isn't any easier than personality-picking in other walks. It's no easier than, say, selecting a spouse among all the eager prancers at a predatory singles bar. Take a look at today's divorce rate if you want an idea of what any lonely-heart VC is up against.

But venture investors stay at it despite the difficulty. They have to. They tell you that their job isn't so much picking companies, concepts, business models, markets, or anything so abstract and obtuse. That's all part of it, of course. But primarily they are making investments in people. When buying into a company, they are creating a partnership, they say, and therefore their first decision-making criterion is the character and personality of their prospective new partners.

The primary one is the chief executive officer. In a young company, the management team is likely to consist of two or three people, or maybe even a handful, depending on its age and stage. But the CEO usually is the person who conceived the new business idea. Therefore he is the most passionate about it, and he very likely persuaded the other team members to join in what he considers his certain success. Ultimately, the CEO's shoulders must carry the company. He has to be intelligent and creative enough to produce marketable goods out of raw ideas. He has to be persistent, dedicated, and driven enough to ride a new business over its inevitable bumps. He has to be humble enough to recognize errors and correct them. He has to be aggressive enough to demand more growth and better results even when growth and results appear comfortably adequate. All the while he must maintain morale and optimism within the aspiring organization. And it's nice if he can also remain agreeable while exchanging phone calls with his venture investor, and maybe even catch him up on progress and problems over an occasional beer. VCs much prefer to invest in people they get along with. "I don't care how good the concept is or the market is, if I don't like the guy I don't want to do the deal," says John Fisher of Draper Fisher Jurvetson. "Life is too short."

So a successful entrepreneur has to be a nice guy in addition to demonstrating the leadership qualities of Thomas J. Jackson, the "Stonewall," sitting boldly astraddle his mount at First Manassas. The expectations are very high.

"Entrepreneurs do things that are unnatural acts, things that shouldn't happen," observes Rick Burnes of Charles River Ventures. "They just make things happen. They will them to happen."

Says John Fisher: "A business is nothing but a collection of people. Those are your assets, and if those aren't the highest quality people, then you're not going to have the highest quality results."

Venture capitalists discover some of those highest quality people among the entrepreneurs and wanna-bes who call on them to hustle up cash for their new companies. But that's the exception. Most often a start-up's founders must move out as lead executives—if not right away, then after a company achieves some mass and momentum. Managing larger concerns simply requires separate skills than those needed to start small ones. On the other hand, when VCs discover a talented start-up artist who's proven he can accelerate an idea into a successful business, they'll reuse him as soon as they can.

That adds up to three ways that venture capitalists find entrepreneurial talent to run the companies they finance: Discover it in the founders. Reuse it when you can. Import experienced managers when you have to. No matter which approach they follow, VCs take pains to make sure the companies they back are backed by people who are capable, adroit, and astute.

That can't be very far from the first principle for any investment: Back good people. It certainly applies to buying stock in a publicly traded company. Or to buying into mutual funds, for that matter. Who's running the show? When Peter Lynch managed the fabled Magellan Fund for Fidelity Investments, he became a finance star for the returns he garnered. Following the leader, consumers made Magellan the most popular mutual fund in its heyday. Fidelity rewarded Lynch—while it rode his reputation—by sticking him into television ads as a white-haired, prime-time pitchman for the investment house. That may not have been the wisest decision. Lynch's presentation, physique, and physical demeanor are only a tad more inspiring than those of, say, Bill Gates, who aired in a few, squeaking, feel-good endorsements of his embattled Microsoft at about the same time.

If there's a lesson in that, it's that business leaders don't have to be telegenic. General Electric won't suffer if Jack Welch never makes an ad—although it's a good bet the effervescent, energetic little CEO would present himself better than either Lynch or Gates.

General Electric is a blue chip that habitually lands very near the top of the Fortune 500. No doubt the barkers in its investor relations office can trot out limitless statistics meant to show that GE has always done well for its stockholders. And they'll make all the standard arguments about how the company will continue to be a solid investment under whatever future, unnamed regime takes over when Welch retires as planned in April 2001. But still the questions will come up about a successor to the chairman and chief executive officer.

That's because no one really questions that Jack Welch—officially it's John F. Welch, Jr.—is the dynamo who has powered General Electric's bright rise during the two decades he has served at its head. Lately its been called the last conglomerate, and it's easy to argue that present-day General Electric is an enormous extension of its boss's enormous personality. While many other widely diffused corporate behemoths have shed unassociated businesses and struggled to establish a coherent and cohesive line of commerce, GE has traveled in the other direction. It has heaped together a collection of disparate operating units that range over jet-engine manufacturing, electrical generators, lightbulbs, railroad locomotives, high-performance plastics, credit, and equipment leasing. GE's empire even includes the NBC television network. Under the short, tireless, cocksure, and irrepressible Jack Welch, General Electric takes in $120 billion annually and routinely reports double-digit earnings growth.

Savvy stock pickers have rewarded Jack Welch's GE by bidding up equity prices more than 500 percent since 1995 alone. But recognizing the importance of solid leadership, investors also don't hesitate to withdraw support as soon they begin to doubt the top dog. Both professional money mangers, who buy and sell large blocks of stocks, and Wall Street analysts, whose views influence a lot of purchases, have been known to wield their clout to short-circuit the career of any CEO they doubt. Coca-Cola flourished during the sixteen-year reign of Roberto C. Goizueta, who became chairman and chief executive in 1981. But M. Douglas Ivester, who took the job upon Goizueta's passing in late 1997, raised doubts. The company's stock value drifted downward from $77 per share at the close of the first quarter 1998, to $48 by the time the third quarter of 1999 closed. In April 2000, Ivester packed up his desk. In another instance, glamorous Jill Barad became a toy-industry idol because she sold a lot of Barbie dolls for Mattel. But she proved less adept at maneuvering the whole unwieldy company when she moved in as chairwoman and chief executive. Mattel's stock price fell like Niagara in October 1999. Barad exited on February 3, 2000.

Any commercial undertaking rises or falls on the strength of its leaders. New ventures included. You could even make the case that for start-ups, solid leadership is even more essential. A corporate giant has the mass and momentum to keep stumbling forward when executives misstep. Small companies are a lot less likely to find their way home without a good guide.

"When I first got involved in the venture business, I did an analysis across Crosspoint's portfolio, trying to answer the question: All right, how does this work?" recalls Seth Neiman. That was in 1994, when he was still thinking about taking a job at Crosspoint Venture Partners. Thoughtful, analytical, thorough, and precise—yet with a subtle playfulness that asserts itself within his workday rigors—Neiman joined as an associate in 1994, becoming a general partner in 96. Today he is managing partner. "I learned that the only high correlation with the success of a business was the quality of the CEO. Even if they had great markets and great technology, there were no successful companies that didn't also have a great CEO. And there were CEOs who, despite being handicapped with smaller markets and other kinds of problems, found a way to be successful. There are some great stories here—not necessarily that I'd want them published—of CEOs who were dealt the worst possible hands, but they turned them into great companies."

That doesn't mean the right personality alone will account for a good investment. VCs very carefully look at other factors as well when they consider a new company. Fisher puts the selection criteria in an ordered ranking that begins with the people involved. Next comes the target market, including its size, its growth rate, and its competitive landscape, which can include both the number and size of the contenders involved, and their ferocity. Third is the business model a prospective company is based on. The interest in business models is to shy away from entries into low-margin businesses with unpredictable revenue streams that demand a lot of capital for, say, slow-paying manufacturing plants. The favored models return high margins. They have the prospect for high growth that can be sustained internally, by factors under the company's control—perhaps by introducing new product variations.

They pay predictable and recurring revenue streams. Number four in Fisher's priorities is the technology involved. The Internet has made that a more distant concern, he says in a view that's echoed at a lot of other venture practices. That's because many Internet start-ups aren't developing technology. They're probing for creative ways to use what's already created. But a lot of venture deals also still focus on technology breakthroughs. In fact, the Internet itself stimulates a lot of development in newer, better equipment for communications networks. In such technology plays, VCs want ideas that are unprecedented. It's nice, too, if a breakthrough is so unique, it can create a technological dependence, and even a proprietary product position, whereby customers have to stick with a product like addicts, the way computer users once had to take Windows upgrades from Microsoft. It guarantees continuing revenues.

While those basic elements of an investment review remain pretty constant from firm to firm, not everyone agrees on their order. Don Valentine says that when the founders of Cisco Systems first shopped for venture capital back in the 80s, a number of Silicon Valley firms turned them down due to doubts about the leaders. Those VCs looked at personality first when considering a yea or a nay for an investment. Sequoia Capital had the same doubts, claims Valentine, but it funded Cisco, anyway. "We had the advantage of understanding the product and the market for the product, from other investments," Valentine says. Still, Sequoia's backing came with a stipulation meant to mitigate the risk of inadequate leadership. "We financed it because we knew the market was spectacular, and because we had an agreement with the founders to bring in management," says the VC.

"The addressable market is always the number one issue," asserts Scott Tobin, a partner at Battery Ventures, a bicoastal that operates out of Wellesley, near Boston, and out of Silicon Valley's San Mateo. "You can always switch out a team, and it happens. But you can't create a good market if it's a bad market. And you can't have an extremely large company in a small market." Battery wants big companies. "We go into every investment saying we want to make at least ten times our money," says Tobin. "That's not to say that each of our investments makes it, but that's the goal."

The view doesn't diminish the importance of personality. It just acknowledges that the right persons to run a company may not be the ones who originally walk in the door with it. When Battery backed Akamai Technologies in September 1998—a deal that turned out to be one of the coveted ten-baggers Tobin seeks—the venture firm had already taken steps to top the organization with proven professional managers. "In order to consider it a viable investment, it needed to have what I would consider adult supervision," Tobin says. "There was a very, very large market they were going after, but the team was somewhat immature." He's not knocking the three founders of Akamai, an Internet content service that helps other Web businesses improve their speed, reliability, and Web site content—a handsomely large market when you consider all the companies trying to turn heads and attract buyers to their on-line facilities. But the founders' prowess was in technology, not business management. All three came from MIT. All three remain in executive board roles at Akamai. Tom Leighton is chief scientist. Daniel Lewin is chief technology officer. Jonathan Seelig, who was still an MBA student when the trio first appeared at Battery's doorstep, is vice president of strategy and corporate development.

To run business operations, Battery first recruited Paul Sagan, who was already known to Battery, and who was known to be shopping around for a management job. Sagan has new-tech background that blends entrepreneurial exploits with management experience at Big Inc. He was a founder of RoadRunner, a high-speed cable modem service tying computer users to the Internet, and of Pathfinder, a Web company said to be a pioneer in Internet advertising. On the corporate side, he worked as president of Time Inc. New Media, and he was managing editor of Time Warner's *News on Demand*. Tobin introduced Sagan to Akamai before Battery had even committed to finance the company—both for Sagan to get acquainted, and to tell Tobin what he thought of Akamai as an investment opportunity. Sagan liked the opportunity so much, he

signed on as president and chief operating officer a few months before Battery even wrapped up its due diligence. Later, about six
months after Battery made its first-round infusion, George Conrades joined as chairman and chief executive. Once an IBM corporate manager, Conrades had been chief executive of BBN, the software company that put together ARPAnet, the early foundation for
the Internet. After BBN sold to GTE in 1997, he headed GTE Internetworking. Conrades first encountered Akamai as a VC with Polaris Venture Partners, which invested in the start-up two months
after Battery, in November 98.

But even before the chairman climbed aboard, Battery's Tobin
was busy hiring key managers to join the president, Paul Sagan. He
brought in a controller, recruiting him from another Battery portfolio company that had just been sold. He found a vice president of
marketing strategy by working the Rolodex, identifying a good
candidate through professional contacts. When all was said and
done, the venturers had built an entire corporate structure around
the technical core created by the company's founders.

"When we set this up it was three guys in a bathtub," says Tobin.
"I found them office space at 201 Broadway," in Cambridge, Massachusetts, near the university. "They brought the entire lab over
from MIT. If you had walked in at three o'clock in the morning at
MIT, they would have been there doing their thing. We moved the
people one block away, and at three o'clock the next morning they
were still doing it, and it made no difference to them whether they
were at MIT or at Akamai. Today they remain the crown-jewels of
the corporation."

Tobin attests that Akamai has proven to be largely a trouble-free
deal. Once the management team was built, it took over without
any baby-sitting by the venture capitalists. Conrades and Sagan are
both well seasoned, after all. But not every investment runs so
smoothly. In fact, not many do. Expecting the unexpected, most
VCs maintain the view that they'll take the best people over the
best idea or the best market.

Henry McCance, the sage of Greylock, presents leadership as the
first principle of successful venture practice. It's the one thing you

have to get right, no exceptions allowed, in order for an investment to succeed. That's nothing new. McCance says the idea was institutionalized at Greylock when Bill Elfers started the practice back in 1965, because it was the most important lesson Elfers took from his mentor, the fabled General Georges Doriot of American Research and Development.

"Doriot used to always say, to paraphrase, give me an A team and a B product idea, or a B team and an A product idea, and I'll take the first every time," intones McCance in his characteristic, careful meter, and with an appreciation for his trade that's scarcely subdued. "I think the reason Doriot evolved to that philosophy and the reason that we subscribe to it is because, even back then and it is more true today, technology is changing so fast. Market opportunities are changing so fast. Often what you invest in may evolve to something quite different over the length of a relationship. So if you have an A team, they will be able to internalize the changes, make the strategic calls that are necessary, and adapt to the changing environment that they're forced to live in."

In other words, it may turn out that the company the venture capitalist ends up with doesn't look much at all like the company he first invested in. William Kaiser, a Greylock partner, tells of an unanticipated about-face by Mainspring CEO John Connolly two years ago that surprised even the board of directors. At that time, in addition to Kaiser, the Mainspring board included VCs Jerome Colonna, cofounder of Flatiron Partners, and Paul Maeder of Highland Capital Partners, which had coinvested with Greylock in Mainspring's first round of funding, in June 1996. Mainspring was humming, with about $5 million on its balance sheet and about three dozen workers, when CEO Connolly recognized on his own that its course and direction were all wrong. He laid off about three-quarters of the company he had founded in April 96, and started again almost from scratch, giving Mainspring its current mission of building e-business strategies as a consultant to Fortune 1000 companies.

"It was John that did the fix," says Kaiser. "Not the board. No one else. A less experienced person would have just said, 'well, this is what I originally told the investors I was going to do. I can't change it.' And so he would have driven the car right off the edge of the cliff. John had enough experience in his bones that he just felt he was going in the wrong direction. There was enough mutual trust and respect between himself and his board that we gave him one-hundred percent support to changing the direction of the company, even though that seemed at the time to be a risky pirouette to make." Connolly's entrepreneurial experience goes back to 1989, when he cofounded Course Technology, a publisher of educational materials. In summer 2000, two years after his remaking of Mindspring, he was traveling the road show promoting the company before its IPO.

Too bad it's not easier to identify that brand of coveted corporate leader. But the fact is, it can be hard for a VC to know in any objective terms even what he's looking for.

"First, is this person a leader," enumerates Rick Burnes of Charles River. "Does he have energy? Does he have conviction? We use the word *compelling*. Is the person a substantial person? Is it a person who is going to do something? Can you say, 'now that's a guy I won't forget'? You know, there are some people who you just aren't going to forget. Because they think for themselves. They have a different slant. They're confident."

That all seems clear enough. But it would be tough to place a finger on any one of those qualities to say for certain, here it is, right here. They're all a little squishy.

The profile becomes somewhat clearer when Burnes summarizes specific business management attributes he seeks. "You look for people who are smarter than your average bear. That's very important, because smart people are quick studies," meaning they'll detect movement before the movement becomes obvious. "We look for honesty. Energy (again). Market vision—somebody who really understands a market. Another characteristic is somebody who listens very carefully, because you can't understand what's going on in a market unless you listen carefully. If you had all those characteristics in spades, we'd back you."

Nancy Schoendorf, in picking entrepreneurs for Mohr Davidow on the coast opposite Charles River, looks for strategic thinkers. "People who think very strategically and are aware of their market and their customers are able to figure out a path that allows them to continue to build products and services to satisfy customers needs, and grow into a larger and larger company."

But Burnes, Schoendorf, and any other thoughtful VC will also admit that the problem with any leadership formula or attributions list is that either can fail to pick the standouts from the fresh-cut recruits who haven't had experience enough to expose all their qualities. One of Charles River's best management selections, Steven Walske, looked like an enormous risk at the time the firm tapped him to head Parametric Technology, in 1986. His highest management rank had been chief financial officer, for another Charles River investment that didn't fare well. Walske was still in his early thirties. But the firm needed a chief executive who would stand up to Parametric founder Dr. Samuel Geisberg, age fifty-seven at the time, a Russian who had come to the United States via Israel with a breakthrough idea for the software that engineers use to design mechanical goods, like cars and Caterpillar tractors.

Geisberg didn't want to run business operations. He acknowledged the new company needed a professional CEO. But, recollects Burnes, "if we brought in some fifty-six-year-old, technically oriented marketing guy to run the company, it wasn't going to work. We needed somebody who could tell Sam, 'no, you go back and design your products; I'll run the company and sell them.'

"Steve Walske's father was a Princeton physicist, and Steve runs in that crowd intellectually. Even at thirty-three, Steve was very tough minded. And by that I mean that he'll take hard stands. And he was a very independent person. I mean he isn't going to follow the crowd. Even though he was a very young guy, we thought he was tough enough to stand up to Sam. But he wasn't competitive at all with Sam. That was a key factor," Burnes notes.

In 1996, nine years after it was released, Parametric's mechanical engineering software overtook rival products that had once owned the market. Parametric has dominated the segment by a wide margin ever since, growing to become the sixth largest independent software company in the world.

Venture capitalists often talk about employing pattern recognition—the skill whereby you recognize the basic shape and outline of an entity apart from its own, unique particulars. Applied to new-venture investments, the idea is to spot the patterns that have brought success in the past. The details of different deals, after all, are inherently variable. But consistent outlines should emerge.

But in personality profiling, that can be easier said than done, precisely because each situation is so idiosyncratic. At Parametric, for instance, the CEO needed more than just the usual pattern of better-bear qualities. He also had to synch with the peculiarities of Dr. Sam Geisberg, the technical core of the corporation who wasn't going to go anywhere. And Geisberg's peculiarities illustrate another problem: As any bank loan officer, minister, psychologist, battlefield commander, or dating service executive will attest, people are all pretty different, and they're usually pretty tough to assess. When judging qualities of character, you can never be sure what's there until you see a person exercise it.

"One of the things that investing in Agile has taught me is that pattern recognition is not the right way to select executives," says Nancy Schoendorf of Mohr Davidow. She was the first venture capitalist to back the company. But she did it on a hunch, because cofounder Bryan Stolle's resume simply wasn't fat enough to show what kind of a chief executive he would turn out to be. In hindsight, she says, "we could never have hired a better CEO for that company. Had we insisted on doing that, we would not have ended up with such a good outcome."

The perils of personality drive many VCs to recycle, funding proven entrepreneurs who come back for a second or even a third crack at corporate creation. For example, about a third of Charles River's investments go to returning entrepreneurs. (Many others go to second-tier executives from its portfolio companies; they may not have experience running an entire organization, but at least some of their abilities have been on display.) Charles River put money behind Desh Deshpande when he started Cascade Communications in 1990 because it had already observed his talents in 88, when Deshpande had cofounded Coral Networks, another communications-equipment maker. The biggest problem with reuse is that there aren't enough seasoned entrepreneurs to go around, particularly when the competition to fund new companies grows fierce. "They're the hardest people to back, because everybody wants to back them," says Burnes. Tellingly, Charles River isn't in on the funding of Deshpande's latest creation, Sycamore Networks. Presumably some other VCs beat the firm at the table.

At least there are a few systematic ways to start to identify good leaders. It helps to look at the education level a person attained, and the institutions he or she attended. Not that every successful business founder comes from Harvard or Stanford or MIT and that ilk. And not even because Harvard or Stanford or MIT educate their charges any better. But they're choosier about who they let in. Therefore their admissions departments amount to a reliable first filter at least, for gauging basic intelligence. Besides, it takes some determination to get through a demanding university.

There's also a credit check. There can be a peek into law enforcement records to make sure a prospective partner has never been convicted of securities fraud, embezzlement, public intoxication, drug smuggling, manslaughter, murder, or the like. An important formal element of personality testing is a reference check—hunting up associates and acquaintances of the entrepreneur who can give a firsthand account of her character, temperament, stress-handling capabilities, and so on. References can include both those the entrepreneur provides like any other job applicant, and those an intrepid investor uncovers on his own. In fact, a recommendation that arrives unsought from a trusted source can be a valuable first hint about an entrepreneur's abilities. Schoendorf says she first met Stolle through a CEO of a successful company, who suggested she have a look at Stolle's just-hatched plan for Agile. "That made a huge difference," she says. "I get so many business plans every day.

Unless one's been referred to me, I don't even have the time to look at it."

But in the end there is no structured system, pattern, or procedure a venture capitalist can use to reliably ID the best budding business managers. As Sequoia's Donald Valentine points out, it gets down to little more than an investor's sense of smell. "And in all fairness," he says, "you don't want to pre-judge. You want to give everybody the shot they want."

It's certainly easier if you find the right leader out of the box, attached to the company he's promoting. "If in fact you have founders that can grow with the opportunity, it is monumentally easier for us to stay with them and augment them where they modestly need augmentation," says Valentine. "It's monumentally hard to hire a John Morgridge when you're looking for him. It's much easier to finance a company where you have all of these people in place. That almost never happens. But it is very desirable. We finance companies both ways."

The reality runs contrary to the pervasive cultural myth that sees a boy-wonder techno-genius hopping a freight train to Silicon Valley with nothing but an idea in his head and a dream in his heart, turning them both into a commercial empire and managing at the same time to somehow woo Julia Roberts. The reality is a lot closer to the disposition of the two fabled founders of Yahoo, grunge-kids David Filo and Jerry Yang—who, as a version of the legend goes, were living in a trailer when they worked up the Yahoo Internet search engine as a hobby in 1994 while studying for their doctorate degrees at Stanford. They never quite ran the company. Yahoo incorporated in April 95 behind funding from Sequoia, led by VC Michael Moritz, who still sits on Yahoo's board of directors. Within a year, Tim Koogle was on board as president and chief executive officer. He became chairman in 1999. Jeffrey Mallett joined at about the same time as an executive assigned to take Yahoo around the world. He is now president and chief operating officer. Other members of the management team arrived as early, including Anil Singh, senior VP in charge of sales and marketing, and Timothy Brady, senior VP of network services. Farzad Nazem, who joined in 1996, is Yahoo's current computer whiz, serving as chief technology officer. Today cofounder Jerry Yang is a corporate director. His partner David Filo is officially described by the company as a "key technologist." Both are said to be "currently on a leave of absence from Stanford's electrical engineering Ph.D. program." Together Yang and Filo are listed at the top of Yahoo's Web-published roster of corporate officers. Their title: Chief Yahoo. It's very cute, but you have to wonder what they really do.

"You can count on one hand the number of CEOs who have scaled from raw start-up to a multi-billion-dollar enterprise," observes Greylock's Kaiser. "You think of Michael Dell, or Tom Stemberg at Staples, or Scott McNealy at Sun, or Larry Ellison at Oracle. Or Gates, for that matter." But they're the exceptions, no matter how loudly they're celebrated.

Of course, a start-up can still grow quite large, and still be very successful, without demanding that its founders scale up to match a challenge anywhere near as big as running, say, Dell or Oracle. Still, VCs go into a deal anticipating that the founders aren't likely to run their companies forever. "People run out of head room. They run out of gas at some point along the line," says Kaiser. "As a director, and as an investor, your job is to make sure that when that person runs out of gas, you know it before they do, and you either have people within the company who are ready to step up, or you have people outside the company that you can bring in."

"Not a whole lot of the founders stick around or are left in place as CEO," echoes Jim Hynes, the former head VC at Fidelity Ventures. "They're great for starting a company. Their involvement is great when it's an idea and there are eight guys sitting in a garage. But as soon as it gets to an office building, and it gets to 20 employees or 30 people or 40 people, they have no idea how to deal with the complexity. The strategy has to be spelled out and put into writing. There have to be HR policies. There's gotta be this. There's gotta be that. And a lot of times these guys just aren't geared to handle that. Or inclined. I mean, they usually recognize it. They become chief technical officer, or maybe they sit on the board."

John Moores saw it that way in 1987, when he ran BMC Software. "I fired the CEO and replaced him with somebody who was a whole lot better. I was that CEO I fired," he says. Moores did very well with the little software company he bootstrapped by selling computer programs he wrote himself in the late 1970s. Today the former entrepreneur is owner of the San Diego Padres, yet another major league baseball team that enjoys the distinction of having lost a recent World Series to the New York Yankees. At BMC, Moores recognized that his style no longer fit the company he had created. "I made every decision on a gut feel," he explains. "It was management by walking around. I don't like to go to meetings. I don't like to read memos. I'm damn sure not going to write them. The company just got too big."

Still, replacement can become a touchy issue. Contractual authority and control of the board by venture investors often aren't enough to avoid a nasty fight if a founder decides to stay ungracefully. Therefore, VCs like to clear the question before they commit to invest. "An individual can do a lot of damage," rues Schoendorf. "If you have concerns, or you think that replacement might be the outcome, it's very important that you have that conversation with a person, very directly, so that you know what their response is going to be. If you have somebody that you have concerns about, and their response is, 'no, I'm going to be the one who builds this company,' then you'd better think twice before you invest."

That's not meant by VCs to take anything away from the individuals with the ideas. "The founder is the individual who has the brilliance, the vision, the intelligence, the energy to break down the walls to lead a thing to the next level," says venture funder John Fisher. "Oftentimes they don't have the management skills to take it all the way. But sometimes they actually develop the skills."

"There is something very heroic about being an entrepreneur," says Izhar Armony of Charles River. He calls himself a failed entrepreneur, because the company he started in Israel, while still in operation, didn't grow to be a billion-dollar business. As a venture capitalist, Armony likes to joke with Evan Schumacher about a drawing of Don Quixote that hangs in Schumacher's office at Celarix, the company Schumacher founded, and which Armony funded. "I am Sancho Panza," the VC quips. "I have no problem with that. My role is to help heroic people achieve great things."

An entrepreneur is a person apart, with a get-it-done temperament that shows on his office walls and in his workday surroundings just as clearly as the personality and professional circumstances of Jack Welch are written onto General Electric's sixty-acre headquarter's campus in Fairfield, Connecticut. For all its bosky, bucolic charm, the GE site is expertly crafted to convey order, organization, and control. Outside the main administration building, a high wall conceals visitors' cars, as though they're too discordant to be on display. Inside the building's reception area, a block of red-upholstered seats for waiting guests is centered deep within a cavernous room of cool shadows. The message: corporate power confident enough to remain just out of sight.

By contrast, Evan Schumacher's Celarix originally occupied a dingy, yellow-brick building at 254 Friend Street, one block off of Causeway, which is the street fronted by Boston's Fleet Center sports arena. The neighborhood is overrun by the bars, burger joints, and fast-food counters serving the crowds that spill out after Boston Celtics basketball games, after Bruins hockey matchups, after circus acts, ice shows, rock concerts, and other goings-on. Across the street from Celarix's first HQ, Jimmy Mac's pub advertises Budweiser on a shocking green awning that runs fully across its front. Next door stands a place that calls itself Bulfinch Roma—Home of the Big Slice. A banner promises breakfast, lunch, and dinner, but the iron grate over the door is usually padlocked. One balmy night in early April 2000, CEO Schumacher and some other late workers cut out earlier than normal—about 9 P.M.—after a dozen or so police cruisers converged on their street. Best to call it a night, they figured. From news reports the next morning they learned about the knifing outside, involving some of the rag-haired teens who had come to hear a Fleet Center concert of a sort that Schumacher couldn't begin to describe—some variant of trailer trash rock or hip-hop.

Celarix filled all five floors of 254 Friend Street to bursting. Before it moved out in May 2000, eighty workers were sharing three single-seat lavatories. Schumacher had given up his office to make room for four desks. The sacrifice gave Laura McKowen, Celarix's twenty-something marketing director, her first permanent desk. During her first couple of months on the job, McKowen had floated every morning to find an open work space. Intraoffice mobility is one reason why Celarix equips its staff with laptop computers instead of full-blown desktop PCs. Another reason is because employees take work home, and out on the road when they travel.

Even after Celarix moved to its more commodious, just-built offices in neighboring Cambridge, its preferred beverage remains a caffeine-laced concoction called Red Bull Energy Drink. (Its can warns, "Not recommended for children and persons sensitive to caffeine.") The company obtained an import license so it could get cases of the stuff from Austria. Red Bull tastes a little like sweetened tar, which makes it a good companion for washing down the box-loads of Doritos and other chips and quick snacks strewn ready for grabbing on tabletops at through-points throughout the offices. Even the new place is redolent of stale, oniony burgers and greasy pizza, the characteristic scents left by workers who routinely eat at their desks.

Venture capitalists, who often dine very well, love the smell. It signifies the entrepreneurial action they dream of. Schumacher is the brand of leader they hunt for.

5

FILTERING THE HYPE

Good venture capitalists use good judgment.

This chapter could end with that. Or it could run on for a spell citing how, when Don Valentine hired John Morgridge to run Cisco, or, say, when Charles River moved in Steve Walske to counterbalance Sam Geisberg at Parametric, or when Nancy Schoendorf said yes to Bryan Stolle and Agile, they each exercised good judgment. Or it could cite some examples of wise decisions that will be detailed in chapters yet to come, which invoke some of the other investment methods VCs use. Of course, it could just as easily tick through instances of bad judgment—although you won't hear nearly as much about mis-selections from venture capitalists themselves, which is natural. And within the scope of this book that bias is acceptable. After all, this is about how VCs *succeed*.

Still, no matter what you call it, applying good judgment and avoiding bad doesn't belong exclusively to venture capital. It's a fundamental principle that hides beneath the success of any investment. For that matter, it's a foundation of success in any undertaking. Besides, good judgment isn't really an attribute anybody can acquire. It may be sharpened by use, and perhaps dulled by neglect, but still it's hard to imagine a school that could have taught Solomon how to subdivide babies. Some people seem to be simply born with a propensity to see facts clearly no matter how many obscuring circumstances cloud their view. Some bright folks can simply avoid being duped into a bad decision. What more can you say?

But as difficult as it might be to fit into any discussion about venture investing principles, the exercise of judgment is also very awkward to avoid. For one thing, it's too fundamental to hide. Care and judgment show up very clearly in the day-to-day decisions of consistently successful VCs. For another thing, it's an attribute that can sometimes get lost, even in people who appear to legitimately possess it. Therefore, even the wise must occasionally reprise.

The dotcom investment bubble that by all indications had burst by mid-2000 no doubt caught some people who should have known better. It also made a lot of people only look wise—at least for a while. As long as hyped-up public investors were willing to feed like piranhas on any Web stocks tossed their way, venture capitalists backing new dotcoms couldn't lose.

"In this environment, many people tend to get confused between being smart, and being lucky," quips Izhar Armony, the Charles River partner, speaking when the Nasdaq Internet bubble was still inflated.

But not every VC got caught. Some stand-out firms that even call themselves Internet investors avoided the worst of the carnage by avoiding the segments of Web business that in their judgment looked hollow. Even when colleagues appeared to be winning both fortune and fame, they stayed away from Internet action on the business-to-consumer side of the Web. Dubbed B-to-C—or, in hip cyber-speak, B2C—it includes all the e-tailing enterprises with Web sites that seemed to displace Budweiser during every available television ad gap in the 1998 football season, including the January 99 Super Bowl. It includes Boo. It includes Toysmart. They're the companies that were supposed to lure shoppers out of Wal-Mart, Sears, and Saks during the 99 holiday shopping season. They're the advertisers that were conspicuously absent during the January 2000 Super Bowl.

B2C dotcoms include more than just retail Web sites. And there's little doubt that some of them will turn out to be sustained and successful businesses. Amazon may still chalk up losses, but already it is very firmly situated within the cultural landscape. And for a couple of days in middle July 2000, the consumer Web directory Yahoo energized the entire stock market by reporting record sales for its second quarter that ended June 30. Some venture capitalists will win very handsomely with their B2C investments. But it's also now widely recognized that investors propped up too many, and many of questionable merit.

"You have to be disciplined enough to sit on your hands and listen to all the *yin-yang* that goes on when a fad is in its hot phase, when you look kind of stupid because you don't have any plays there," relates Jim Swartz of Accel Partners. "But rather than trying to follow and jump in on the latest fad, we try to be pretty rigorous in how we think, and in sorting out a fad from a real business direction."

Accel took issue with B2C businesses that bet their success on the notion that they would make scads of money by selling other businesses the waving, flashing, blinking banner ads that still festoon many sites.

"We refused to do any businesses that were based on advertising," says Swartz. "If you looked at the business models these guys were advocating, they just didn't hold water."

A business model encompasses the fundamental rules of commerce a company applies to make its hay. That's different from a business plan, which is the detailed strategy and execution map that a hopeful entrepreneur shows to a VC to convince the investor that his concept is a winner. Business plans lay out specifics like product differentiation, marketing, sales and distribution approaches, and revenue targets. The business model is more fundamental.

One hundred years ago in America, when a lot of little start-ups were jostling to become General Motors and Ford, an auto company's business model might have read: Make cars. It didn't go near the issue of selling cars. That's how enormous enterprises like automobile manufacturers came to rely on independent dealers to represent them to consumers. In some ways, the business model has merit. It liberates the carmakers from the very expensive burden of building and then operating a wide-ranging dealer channel. On the other hand, if you're a domestic manufacturer, the preponderance of competitive, independent car dealers invites offshore rivals to invade your turf, since they don't have to invest in sales facilities, either. The aggressive, competitive, well-financed independent dealers are very happy to do that for them. Even worse, it attaches car companies to faces that insist on appearing in their own local television commercials, and on hiring salespeople who in another era may have mixed snake oils. Basically, it disconnects the manufacturers from car buyers. Because of the mixed-up business model underlying the auto industry, carmakers think of car dealers as their customers, rather than looking at drivers that way. Business models matter a lot.

The problem some discerning VCs saw in the models behind Web-tailers is that the brick-and-mortar storefronts they emulate are simply low-margin commodity businesses that earn only a pittance per sale. "It's not going to take over the world the way everyone was talking about," asserts Rick Burnes of Charles River. "The business models aren't sustainable. There's just no cost advantage, or very little cost advantage. The cost of distribution is too high. It's not a very good business. It was a lot of hype."

That's not to say these same discerning venturers aren't bullish on the Internet. Seth Neiman of Crosspoint Venture Partners posits, "Is Amazon an interesting business? Oh yeah. I mean, it is symbolic of an enormous change that's going on here. Let's be clear here: this is Venice in the twelfth century. World trade is being re-invented.

"But we want to build sustained value over a long period of time," says Neiman about his firm. "And we said, the B-to-C world doesn't seem like it's going to provide that. I mean, if it's a bad business off-line—meaning low margins and low customer retention selling books or CDs or consumer electronics—then once the enthusiasm for the reinvention of the business goes away, it will still be a cruddy business."

In fact, Accel, Charles River, Crosspoint, and some others all herald on-line trade as an unprecedented opportunity for venture capital. But they see the action not in headline-grabbing B2C, but in the hardware and software needed to build and to operate the Internet, and in high-value business services delivered via the Net—the segment called business-to-business, or B-to-B, or, of course, B2B.

For example, at Crosspoint, says Neiman, "we very consciously said we will invest in Internet infrastructure of several different kinds, and then, as that infrastructure gets deployed, we think it will cause the reinvention of business, of B-to-B. And that's what we've been up to. We started with network equipment companies: Digital Island, Foundry, Juniper, Brocade. We went to wide-area and broad-band related companies: Avanex, Efficient, Com21, Sonoma. We went from there to the companies that bought that gear to deploy competitive new networks: Covad, Blue Star, DSL.Net. And now that those things have come out, we're focused almost entirely on B-to-B."

Business services delivered on-line present a more alluring business model. They provide essential corporate services that every company needs. But by delivering them electronically, across the Internet, they provide them more efficiently than conventional methods. That means the business customers subscribing to B-to-B services can save money while they run faster. Businesses will spend greedily for the opportunity to cut costs and gain efficiency. On the other hand, consumers are more interested in saving a dime.

"With B-to-B, you save your customer a lot of money, rather than costing them money," echoes Burnes. "So you have a customer who wants to buy, opposed to a buyer who's reluctant."

Similar judgments make Charles River wary of med-tech investments.

"Healthcare is fundamentally a very difficult area to invest in, because people don't want to spend the money," Burnes explains. The field may have a lot of other encouraging ingredients for private-equity plays, like technological dependence and the opportunity to carve out proprietary product positions. But with the overweening concern to spend less, rather than more on medical care, the buying, says Burnes, will never turn profligate enough to support high venture returns.

For all its value, good judgment doesn't guarantee that a careful VC won't sometimes get pinched. He can also suffer some retribution for suspending good judgment for what seemed like good reasons at the time. Times change.

Rick Burnes won't name the company involved, but he tells of wrangling in a power struggle to place a chief executive in an investment where the founder is fighting it. "He's very chippy. He's got a big ego. He's a classic, salesman blowhard," says Burnes without much restraint. "He's paranoid. He thinks every move you make is meant to undermine his authority. Everyone around him is afraid. They never quite know where they stand."

But he was fine, says Burnes, for the original business plan. When Charles River funded the company in 1999, the aim was to develop the product because of its promising technology, and then sell the company to a larger concern, somebody like Cisco, which routinely refreshes its technology base by buying new ideas that come up from the entrepreneurial groundswell. "We would go into a thirty-million valuation and a year later or two years later sell it in a half-billion dollar valuation," says Burnes. Thus Charles River bought into the deal despite its misgivings about the founder.

But, says Burnes, "in the year that we've been investors, we've learned that the product has much bigger potential than we thought. It's got a bigger market. The company has the capability of being a public company." That would pay a much higher return than the fast-pass sale originally planned. "But there's no question about it: this fellow doesn't have the judgment to run a public company."

To make the holding palatable as an IPO, Burnes explains, "we're at present trying to find a CEO. But this character is resisting us mightily. Egos play a very large role in this." The most likely scenario: The board of directors, which is controlled by Charles River and its venture-capital coinvestors, will boot the founder upstairs to the chairmanship; as of this writing, he's the company's president. As chairman—"which doesn't mean anything," notes Burnes—he'll be given a token assignment that reports to the CEO, who's yet to be hired. But the VC remains hopeful on that front. "I'll bet we'll find a good guy, because there's huge potential. And the first time this other guy gets out of line, we'll fire him."

"We went in with one expectation," which changed, defends Burnes. That's not quite the same as a misjudgment. Still, here's the lesson from that situation and from the late Web hysteria: When it comes to investing, successful venture capitalists don't just have good judgment. They make sure they use it.

6

ROLLING UP THEIR SHIRTSLEEVES

It's hard to imagine a venture capitalist going deeper into the management of a start-up than James P. Hynes went into Colt Telecommunications. He started it. Then he ran it for a year before bowing out as CEO, though he stayed on as chairman for another two years, conferring over high-level strategy and giving the company a face on the Street.

To Hynes, doing it yourself was a way to beat the very costly competition for start-ups, which started when eager VCs with money to spend began bidding up the valuations of entrepreneurial companies. To play in the new-venture game, you have to pay market rates or better to own a piece of a promising company. Or, as Hynes realized, you can start a promising company yourself, and own it all outright.

Hynes first came to Fidelity Investments in 1989 not as a venture investor but as the executive in charge of its telecommunications operations—a big job, since Fidelity performs all of its selling, marketing, and customer support on the network, either on-line or over the telephone. Just prior, he had served as the telecom chief at New York's Chase Manhattan Bank, a job that turned out to be the cap on a twenty-year stint in communications operations and management.

He ran the phones for less than a year at Fidelity before sidling into venture investing. He had no training or experience in the trade. Nevertheless, the bosses at Fidelity thought he could capitalize on the opportunities for nimble, small companies in telecommunications services and equipment that were opening up as a prolonged consequence of deregulation. Six months after the move into venture capital, he became managing director of Fidelity's entire, small-business seek-and-find operation, called Fidelity Ventures.

"They said that I was wasting my time on the operations side, and that I should be building and running companies," he recounts. Hynes is self-assured, jovial, good-natured, and quick to laugh. That helps explain why he doesn't quite come off as imposing or intimidating, even at six feet seven inches tall and 270 pounds. Swap the penny loafers for a pair of Reeboks and he could be atop a lawn tractor, self-absorbed as he idly grooms a green manse—something he has more time for now. At the start of 2000, he retired from Fidelity at age fifty with all the money he might ever want or need. "I kept a promise to myself that if I made enough money, I'd stop working—at least for now." He plays a lot of golf. He's window-shopping for Aston Martins. He sits on some boards and makes some angel bets.

At Fidelity, Hynes took his first shot at from-scratch venture capital in 1990 with Advanced Mobil Communications. Fidelity operated the company, which provided two-way radio service to outfits like construction companies and taxi fleets, which need to stay in touch with roving vehicles. Advanced Mobil operated in smaller cities, in what's called the secondary market. The major metro airwaves were already tied up by an outfit named Fleet Call. For Hynes it was kind of an early take on the concept of incubation, except that instead of just setting the wheels of a new company aturning, he ran operations, serving as chairman and chief executive of Advanced Mobil. The plan was to operate at a profit while expanding aggressively, to saturate the secondary markets until Advanced Mobil became sizable enough to become a plum acquisition, probably by its big-city rival. "Always operate a company as profitably as you can, and then look for a way out if you're not going to be number one or number two," opines Hynes. The view is at odds with the Amazon approach to building a business, which is to spend with abandon until you're so enormous that nobody can challenge you, and then figure out a way to make money.

But at Advanced Mobil at least, the pre-Internet strategy prevailed. Chunks of the company merged with Fleet Call, which went on to become present-day Nextel, the fast-growing wireless communications carrier that provides digital cellular voice and data services throughout the United States and around the world. Sources inside Fidelity say the company netted about $100 million on the deal, three times its $35 million investment. "In the late eighties and early nineties, you were happy with three times or four times your money," says Hynes.

Colt Telecommunications Group of London, England, was by far a bigger deal. As with Advanced Mobil, Hynes served as chairman and CEO of Colt its first year, with another American, Paul Chisholm, seated as president and chief operating officer. Colt began as a fiber-optic network offering local-exchange phone service, competing against the London old guard. Historically the city had been tied up by two telephone companies. "We were the first ones in with an alternative to the duopoly. So we had first-mover advantage," says Hynes. In April 93, four days after the city approved the new company's license, "we started digging up the streets of London. We had done the leg-work in advance. Our first customer was serviced in October 1993." That's the speed of entrepreneurial hunger.

Hynes stuck with his established pattern: After about a year as chief executive, he turned the operation over to Chisholm, but remained on as chairman for a while. Colt now operates phone services in nearly thirty cities throughout Europe. When it went public in December 1996, Fidelity still owned 75 percent of it. From an initial Fidelity investment of $100 million, the phone service has reached a market capitalization peak of $20 billion.

Hynes's activities at Colt show how intimately a venture capitalist can become involved in an investment to steer it toward success.
It's extreme. In most cases, VC involvement is more removed, with
operational management left to the entrepreneurs at a company.
And it was also somewhat of a special case. Fidelity, which isn't a
giant among venture firms, also isn't a typical venture operation.
It's fully funded and controlled by its parent, an arrangement that
can give it some leeway to approach investments a little differently.
For one thing, the guy at the top, Fidelity Investment's Edmond
"Ned" Johnson, has inculcated a do-it-yourself ethos throughout
the organization, which is said to grow from his belief that no one
else can do it as well as Fidelity can. Probably because of that corporate hubris, Fidelity Investments was prepared to foot the entire
bill for Colt, so that Hynes didn't need a financial partner to share
the costs. Besides, backing someone else's company might have
ended up costing the investment house about as much as it ended
up paying, anyway, even though it would have then received only a
share of the start-up. "There was vast amounts of money coming
into venture capital, and pricing [for small companies] was moving
higher and higher," Hynes says. "There was more money chasing
too few deals," a situation that he says grew to be obscene by the
end of 1999.

Still, it illustrates exactly how high a VC's sleeves can roll. Jim
Hynes wasn't dabbling with Colt or playing absentee CEO. He
wrote the corporate strategy. Along with Chisholm he put together
the license application, schmoozed it through to approval, negotiated with contractors to lay the cable, dickered with equipment
makers to supply hardware, and hired the company's key, early employees. "We found fifteen or twenty people who worked like dogs
in a small room," says Hynes. He tells how the first Colt cadre labored in the cramped basement of a London building lent by Fidelity. The conditions proved a rite of passage for the formational
crew. "The most important thing in any company is to find good
people who match up with your value system and your mode of operation. That was critical, and probably the thing we did best."

Investor involvement is a defining practice of venture capital. It distinguishes the field as a craft as much as a profession, because the participation by a VC in a portfolio company depends upon a personal, individual relationship that makes each investment a special case. Each portfolio company has its own particular needs. Peculiar circumstances arise from the unique situation of each. Each relationship has its own particular dynamic, largely defined by the personalities of the people involved.

"It's very specific to a company," concurs Nancy Schoendorf, the Mohr Davidow partner. "It's specific to the problems and the issues they face, and to their needs. And different venture firms work in different ways. We are very hands on, but we're mostly hands-on in about the first 12 months of a company's existence, because if you don't get it right then, it's pretty hard to fix. After 12 months, you get in when there are special reasons."

In general, involvement is the direct, tradesman-like application of specialized skills to an investment to help assure its success. The way it works out, an active venture capitalist basically provides beck-and-call business consulting to his portfolio investments. And he charges no hourly fee. Still, these value-added services are not free. They're part of the package entrepreneurs get when they give up a portion of their company. It's an essential ingredient of venture capital, because the success of its holdings—young companies—is so tenuous and unassured that they wouldn't make suitable investments without the help of experts to boost their odds. Their hands-on participation and involvement make VCs company builders as much as they're financiers.

Investor involvement is a venture principle that is hard to map in other investment classes. It has a clear correlation in real estate, where a developer or even just a property owner can always improve a plot or parcel to increase its value. But buying some shares in Ford Motor Company isn't going to give anyone authority to dip his hands in the automaker's internal operations to make things run better. The scattered scions of assembly-line worker Henry Ford can keep control of his company by holding on to a lot of stock.

One rule of thumb today says that family heirs of a large company's founder can control its board if they retain at least about 10 percent of its stock. Outside of that, weighty investment professionals can affect stock prices by buying a lot of shares or unloading a lot. But that only signals approval or disproval. They can't take any direct, concerted action. They can't, say, plant the great-grandson of an industrial innovator as chairman of the board just because his name is William Clay Ford, Jr.

On the other hand, personal involvement plays a pivotal role in the investment strategy of a successful VC. He spends far more time inside existing investments than he does making new ones. Some VCs report that as many as three-quarters of their extended workday hours go to working with portfolio companies, with each partner in a firm responsible for handling six or eight or ten or more. "Most of my day is dedicated to working with entrepreneurs," illustrates Izhar Armony, the partner with Charles River Ventures. "For us, it is something like 70 percent of our time [that] is spent on current investments. We don't do lots of prospecting."

Venture capital firms buy into fledgling companies under the proviso that their lead investor—the general partner who heads up the particular investment for the firm—becomes a coach and counselor to the entrepreneurs who remain in charge of day-to-day operations.

VCs categorize this involvement under the vague and expansive term "value-add," as in value-added services. It signifies that a venture capitalist brings more than just finances to a bargain. As important as adequate capitalization may be to a young company—to give it spending room to hire staff, lease facilities, procure equipment and supplies, launch business operations, and so on—a VC doesn't just drop the dough on an entrepreneur's desk and then leave those activities for him to figure out. The venture funder also participates, lending his experience and expertise to the undertaking, thereby increasing its value.

Astute entrepreneurs notice that. Many shop for it.

"We wanted VCs on our side who had real money at stake, and who had been involved in both the very biggest technology stories and the very worst technology failures [Benchmark failed to get off the ground with the ballyhooed Toysrus.com, a partnership with the kiddie retailer], who had seen it from both sides," says Robert Young, Red Hat Software cofounder and chairman of the board. Red Hat was four years old by the time Benchmark Partners and Greylock arrived with venture backup in 1998. It already enjoyed some name-brand recognition and a healthy, rapidly expanding customer count that at the time was bringing the company about $11 million in revenue. "We weren't desperate for money," says Young, who joined with Marc Ewing to cofound Red Hat in 1994. "We were running the business on the strength of our cash flow, and I did not want to get into bed with somebody who didn't have vision." What he wanted were venture partners who could bring the company the business knowledge it needed to leap to a higher level. "Instead of Marc Ewing and myself sitting back and saying, 'look at what a good job we've done, we don't need any help,' we did just the reverse. We said, 'look what we've been able to do, but now our opportunity is to scale this thing globally.' Neither of us were arrogant enough to think that we had the experience or the training to be able to seize the opportunities we could see in front of us." One of the venturers' first moves was to recruit a seasoned president and chief executive, Matthew Szulik.

Generally, the term "value-add" means hands-on, side-by-side participation in hiring, planning, and strategic decision-making. In some cases, firms institutionalize value-added services as a sort of business-assistance package available to portfolio companies. For example, some venture practices have recently hired marketing and PR specialists to be shared by the start-ups the firms support. But value-add also includes a lot of unstructured, ad hoc activity that a venture partner undertakes on the fly, in response to arising problems and opportunities. In both cases, it can involve them in issues like how to improve a product, when to alter a marketing approach, or whom to hire for key management slots. It can also in-

clude the ouster and replacement of a CEO, which is a personnel issue at the most fundamental level.

The formal assurance of VC influence comes as a spot on the
company's board of directors. VC control comes through control of
the board, which is commonly managed by coinvesting venture
firms that together occupy the majority of seats—if they agree to
coordinate their efforts. In addition to the board's structure, other
provisions may be negotiated in advance of an investment, specify-
ing certain conditions and criteria that the company must meet. A
common one is the condition that a new CEO be recruited in cases
where the investors foresee that more seasoned, professional managers are needed to help assure a holding's growth and success.

There is no standard approach to packaged value-add. Some
firms don't offer any. Others have institutionalized some services
they think every start-up will need—and that they promote in their
efforts to attract promising entrepreneurs who recognize the need.
Marketing, publicity, and promotion are hot areas, since start-ups
need to get attention quickly if they hope to survive in the noisy,
rapidly changing technology marketplace. Starting in 1989, Mayfield Fund contracted with Jennifer Jones to work with its portfolio
companies, giving them lessons in the strategic importance of marketing and public relations. In September 2000, the thirty-one-year-
old venture house made her a permanent staff member, with the title marketing partner. "I'll do much more value-added service work
than I have in the past," Jones said of her move from for-hire consultant to full-time staffer. In both cases, Mayfield pays the tab for
the consulting Jones provides to its portfolios. The venture firm
also provides an on-staff headhunter to help with executive recruit-
ment, another popular value-added service. Similarly, in April
2000, Sequoia Capital hired Mark Dempster to help its companies
build a brand identity. Additionally, Sequoia employs April King as
its designated human capitalist, a specialist in staffing and recruit-
ment. She helps first-time founders assemble full-blown management teams, advising them on corporate organization and work
flow and the like.

Mohr Davidow Ventures employs five venture partners to serve as white knights to its portfolio interests. They are not investing general partners. Rather, each works as a specialized management consultant, using his own business experience to fill gaps at portfolio companies. The best known among them is Geoffrey Moore, author of the best-selling books *Crossing the Chasm* and *Inside the Tornado*. About once a year he gives each of Mohr Davidow's companies a thorough going-over in the areas of market development and business strategy. The venture firm calls the treatment "Geoffing" their companies. "On our nickel, Geoff comes in and gets their strategy aligned and gets the management team all pointed together behind the same strategy," says Schoendorf, the Mohr Davidow general partner.

The firm's other venture partners operate on a more sustained basis inside individual companies—while on the payroll of Mohr Davidow. They may work as acting CEO, acting VP of engineering, business developer, marketing chief, what have you. Just after joining Mohr Davidow in 1998, venture partner Donna Novitsky spent two to three days each week in San Jose at Datasweep, serving as vice president of marketing for the manufacturing software company. She had just joined Mohr Davidow from the enterprise software supplier Clarify, where, as vice president of marketing for eight years, she had contributed to its growth from an eleven-person start-up in 91 to a $100 million international concern employing 450 staffers. Datasweep founder Vladimir Presyman needed that kind of experience when he started with Mohr Davidow. "He had more of a technology background," Schoendorf explains. "He had put together a great technology team. He knew exactly what the market needed and what he had to build. But he didn't really have the business experience about everything else that he would need to do: how he would evolve a business around it, how he would introduce it, how he would market it." Novitsky brought that expertise. But she didn't just impart it at Datasweep; she employed it. She called on future customers, set up the data operation that would support marketing and sales, and eventually she hired a permanent marketing vice president for the company. "Now he has a strong team. He has one of the best VPs of marketing in our portfolio. He has a terrific sales force and VP of sales, but it would have been very hard for him to get all that going without help," Schoendorf states.

At the same time, it might have been very hard for Mohr Davidow to justify investing in a company with such apparent management weaknesses without the confidence that its venture partners could help fix them. Thus as much as it aids the entrepreneurs, the program also lets the VCs sneak in on deals with companies that are still at a very early stage of their development. That makes it a competitive weapon with two edges: the offer of assistance can attract early-stage entrepreneurs, and it enables Mohr Davidow to even consider companies that could look a little too raw to other firms.

But involvement and participation includes much more than the formalized services that venture investors provide their portfolio picks. It includes much more than prearranging management structure, setting up the board of directors, and establishing formal relationships between investors and entrepreneurs. In fact, in the eyes of many VCs, their board seats are more of a default position that assures them a hand and a voice in company affairs just in case an association with a start-up artist goes sour.

As in personality picking, the activities that go on outside of the formal processes really define VC involvement. And that definition gets tough to pin down, because the activities are always different, and they're very unpredictable. They're provided beyond any packaged services, usually by the lead investor who's responsible for interacting with a particular portfolio pick.

"You never know until you get into a company what the relationship is really going to be like," reflects Jacqueline Morby of TA Associates. "Some companies bring you right in and say, okay, these are our problems. This has happened. I'd like to talk to you about this and that. Let's solve this together and so forth. Whereas with some others you feel like a guest at a party. You come to board meetings and you realize that they're preparing it all for you, as if you're the outsider, just as you were before you invested. And you absolutely cannot tell what it will be like before you make an investment. But you'd like to know, because with some companies you would not have made the investment."

She tells of an unusual case in which a chief executive was so insulated by his established advisers that she couldn't break into the circle. Associates like lawyers, accountants, and other such aides "are great when the company has one- or two-million in sales. But when it gets to twenty- or thirty-million in sales, then this is the most successful company they've ever seen. So they think that anything the company does is wonderful." These accidental yes-men can't help an entrepreneur shoulder his company to a higher level. In this particular investment, which was a company she won't name, Morby first tried to enlist other advisers. The CEO wasn't interested in listening. Her next move was to convince his trusted crew to support the changes she wanted. Finally, probably in response to her clatter for some fresh thinking, the company brought its own new addition to the board. The inner circle knew him, since he had supervised a member of the gang at an earlier job. They respected him. And by simple, happy circumstance, he turned out to be very sharp. "He was perfect," says the VC, "because they trusted him. So he was able to make some changes that needed to be made. But otherwise, nothing would have changed. It was just a closed, closed company."

As a consequence of the improvements, the portfolio holding sailed to a public offering, and ended up netting TA about ten times its investment, Morby notes.

Absent any formal rules or clear delineations, involvement is best defined as the sum of activities a VC undertakes to turn a venture toward success, giving an investment any and all the attention it demands, mustering any resource he can command. Most of all it is a hands-on, get-involved attitude that can manifest itself as coaching, counseling, consoling, promoting, advising, insisting, encouraging, cajoling, and mothering. It remains, in most cases, an advisory role.

It puts the venture capitalist on-call, since services can be delivered during board meetings, over dinner, at office visits, and through frequent and repeated telephone calls that may occur several times a day. Whenever.

The juggling that's required can keep VC Michael Linnert—to name only one—glancing at his watch. A general partner at Palo Alto's Technology Crossover Ventures, Linnert is as affable and accommodating as any Midwestern boy lured to Silicon Valley by the pace and vitality of high-tech business. But the pace overfills his calendar, mostly as he attempts to add value to his investments. "The thing that keeps me around every day is the entrepreneurs I work with," he reflects. "I have done a lot of early stage companies, because when you do early-stage stuff, you form a tight relationship and friendship with the CEOs. I'm working with really smart people, and I enjoy tackling the problems as they come along, and the quick feedback that says, hey, you did that right, or, you didn't do that right, and now how do we navigate the waters here?"

As much as VCs may enjoy the adrenaline fixes and the intellectual jigsaws, the demands can spread them so thin that some firms limit the number of boards that partners serve on. At Battery Ventures they get six each. That's meant to give each partner time to provide what the firm calls blue-collar value-add to its portfolio companies. "We get offended by drive-by directors, who show up once a month at board meetings and say hello," says Scott Tobin of Battery. "We're so hands-on, we're like a mini strategy consulting firm, a mini recruiting firm, a mini investment bank and we're a mini PR agency."

Of course, some firms use other methods to prevent VC attention overload. For one, there's Mohr Davidow's venture-partner program, providing experts to get very deeply involved in a portfolio company so that investing VCs don't have to. Besides, limiting directorships doesn't assure that a partner will escape indenture. To conserve his time, Kevin Harvey, a cofounder of Benchmark Partners, passed the lead to Greylock when the two outfits coinvested in Red Hat. Benchmark operates off of Sand Hill Road, whereas

Greylock, as a bicoastal with offices in both Palo Alto and Boston, is much closer to Red Hat's home in Durham, North Carolina. Greylock also has established connections in the area. "I had not intended on taking another board-of-director seat at the time of the investment," Harvey explains. "But over time I found that I was spending board-level time with the company and I greatly enjoyed it." Hence he signed on as a director in October 1999, about a year after Benchmark and Greylock first paired behind the company.

A lot of value-add addresses standard business needs, such as corporate development and marketing. Executive staffing is a big one, since a capable leadership team is considered the foundation of success for a new company. It's also an area where many new-business leaders need outside help.

"Often the chief financial officer of one of these companies is not that capable, and often they don't even understand why a good chief financial officer can help them run their business," illustrates Morby. A holdover CFO many have been fine for a dainty, one-product company. The costs of manufacturing a single product, of marketing it, distributing it, and whatnot, are all pretty visible. But as a product family grows, and short-lived seasonal variations arrive, and distribution stretches out, and more suppliers join the team, and a few partnerships are penned, vital cost and revenue issues grow murky and obscured. It can require a lot more than a Lotus spreadsheet to pick out where the company is overspending, to determine which products are bleeding it, which are the stars, which facilities' investments are paying off, which are the dogs. Many first-time entrepreneurs lack the experience to realize that the company needs to upgrade management capabilities as it grows.

"The VP of marketing that you can attract when you're a start-up is perhaps a different level of talent than the VP of marketing you can attract when you've got $20 million in private capital on your balance sheet, and you're a $15 million dollar company going to fifty," notes Greylock's Henry McCance. "But maybe the CEO doesn't realize that the company has outgrown his co-founder, who was there on day one. A good director with the forest-from-the-trees perspective can say to him, you know, there is a role for Sam in the company. I wouldn't want to lose him. But I really think we have to think about upgrading the function of VP of marketing and business development."

Venture capitalists are so involved with staffing and building management teams that they become closely acquainted with executive recruiting agencies. They encourage their entrepreneurs to do the same.

"It never even occurs to some of them to hire a recruiter to find the best person possible for a slot," observes Morby. "It seems simple, but if you've never done it or don't know about it, you don't think to do it."

Not that professional placement services are always necessary. The personal network of a seasoned venture capitalist already penetrates deep within the managerial class. When Greylock's Bill Kaiser set out to find a chief executive for Red Hat, he didn't have to think hard to come up with Matthew Szulik as an A-list candidate. He knew Szulik from a prior investment. "I picked up the phone and called Matthew," recounts Kaiser. "He was a long-time friend. We got reacquainted and I said, 'I've got an opportunity for you. Would you be willing to listen to it?'" At the time, Szulik was president of Relativity Software, which makes business-management software. Says Kaiser: "I like to joke that I knew one person in the state of North Carolina and it happened to be him. And he happened to be the right guy for the job. That's not too much of an exaggeration."

Henry McCance tells of flying from Boston to New York's La Guardia Airport to interview a candidate for chief financial officer for Trilogy, a software company in Greylock's portfolio. As a board member, McCance had been called on by Trilogy's chief executive to help sell Trilogy to Pat Kelly, who at the time was finance chief of Sabre, the thirty-year-old computer reservation specialist. Kelly faced a dilemma that's common among executives courted by the entrepreneurial sector: Should he leave the security of a well-established company for the high-promise, high-peril realm of business creation? "He could have written his ticket with a number of other companies," says McCance. "I viewed him as having the right personal make-up, the right experience set, knowledge of the Internet and large-company experience that he could bring to Trilogy. So I answered a lot of Pat's questions about whether he should leave this bigger, safer company and take a more entrepreneurial step at this point in his life."

Such simple reassurances can turn out to be a significant contribution from venture investors. Many upstarting companies have little else they can offer to wavering job candidates, wary suppliers, or potential customers. "Often times companies need the venture investor to help sell," says Schoendorf. "They may have identified some great candidates, but to really get people to take that leap, they need the venture investor to be very candid about it. I've had customers call me and ask, 'Why did you invest in this company? Is this company really solid? Are you going to put more money behind it if they need it? Are they really going to be a business?' Our name is there, our reputation is there, and we are there personally to lend credibility to the business."

Outside of the sort of standard-issue assistance that almost every start-up needs to one degree or another, demands and opportunities that arise uniquely for individual investments account for a lot of VC involvement. These special needs can wander pretty far afield. For example, when some pop performers and their entertainment-industry bosses sued Napster in the summer of 2000, trying to shut down the Web site that served as a directory for people who wanted to bootleg recordings among themselves, Hummer Winblad was involved in its portfolio company's defense.

But most of the undefined, ad hoc value-add is less spectacular. It gets into boosterism and encouragement, promotion, strategic counseling, needling, pushing. "There's a lot of blocking and tackling," explains Schoendorf. "It's the silliest things sometimes. It can be introductions to the right firm to help do your PR. They're not things that seem like high value-add, but if you get them right they can be high value-add."

Jacqui Morby has run into entrepreneurs who need extra goading when they become risk averse after a taste of success. The problem appears most often in the later-stage businesses that TA hunts for. "Once a company is up and running, in a way the entrepreneur can begin moving backwards, because, he took a lot of risk at the beginning and now he has something really great and he doesn't want to lose it," she says. But that caution can prevent the company from spending for next-big-step initiatives like, say, expanding internationally or responding rapidly to unanticipated opportunities—or challenges—that arise with changes in technology. "I have sat in meetings and said, 'Why are you not spending the money to do this? It's worth it. Don't worry about spending,'" says Morby. "They know that you invested on a certain financial-performance projection. But, in between time the market may have changed a bit. So we say, 'we don't care that we aren't going to have that $500,000 in profit this year. We'd rather have you do this, so you'll control that market.'"

In 1999, TA invested in a company that promptly needed to hear those assurances repeated over a handful of meetings before it started to remake its software for Web hosting. That's a big step, since it fundamentally changes the way software is delivered and the way the software provider makes money. This company, which Morby doesn't name, writes optical-recognition programming that reads, verifies, and records incoming checks for the Internal Revenue Service, for many state tax offices, and for other organizations like utilities, that take a lot of checks from people. At the time TA bought in, the company delivered its product to buyers the way everyone else in the business had delivered software products for the last two decades or so: written onto disks or CDs as computer code and sold outright. That leaves buyers on their own to run the programming at their facilities, on their own computers. But as a consequence of the Internet, new software companies called application service providers arrived to relieve the headaches and much of the expense of buying and running software for corporate computer users. Application service providers (ASPs) operate the programming for their customers, usually charging a monthly fee, like rent. The procedure is called

Web hosting. With hosted software, customers don't have to dig deep to cover a big purchase price before they've derived any benefit from the product. They pay as they use it. What's more, they don't have to invest in computer hardware to support the system. Finally, and maybe most importantly, they don't have to worry about maintenance, upkeep, and similar recurring expenses that can quickly outstrip the original cost of buying and installing the original code. The ASP does all that. All customers do is travel the Internet to where the software physically resides, on servers at a facility operated by the ASP. Early into 2000, TA's portfolio software company was moving quickly into ASP services, to be sure no competitor beat it to Internet delivery of check-reading systems.

"Now, would they have done that without us?" muses Morby. "Could be. I don't know. But they might not have because they were being very conservative. We met with the CEO about three or four times. We were saying, 'Now, how are you going to get positioned here, and what are you going to do?' This company has always been run very profitably, and I think that they were somewhat worried about spending the money. And we were saying, 'Don't worry about that. You have to move fast. We don't want someone else to get here first.' We could see what was going on. They could too, but they're trying run their own business and it isn't always as easy to realize that they might have someone else come and take that piece away from them," she explains.

"That's what an outside investor does: you're always looking at the broad picture for the business. You're not just looking at the financials and saying, 'well, good job,' or 'why aren't you making more money.' You're trying to look at the more strategic aspects of the business." In this case, the broad picture amounted to knowledge of how quickly software was moving to the application service provider setup. "We were seeing a thousand business plans for ASP models for everything in the world," the VC attests. "What we did was broaden their perspective. You usually find these entrepreneurs so focused on their market and their way of doing business that they don't have a broad view of the world. They're doing well, but they just need a broader view."

Agile Software didn't need a lot of initial help outside of team-building, says Schoendorf. Nevertheless, CEO Bryan Stolle acknowledges the contribution the company gained from the informal, unstructured kibitzing that came from its venture funders.

Agile Software helps manufacturers communicate with suppliers that make vital components used in the manufacturers' products. Sometimes the suppliers can even make the whole product, which the manufacturer brands and sell as its own, an arrangement called "virtual manufacturing." It requires a lot of coordination. In some segments of electronics especially, virtual manufacturing is so pervasive that the ability to quickly and automatically hand off information about product makeup has made Agile Software all but indispensable. But when Stolle and his two partners cofounded Agile in the middle 1990s, their ambitions weren't quite so high. He says Mike Moritz, the venture partner who brought Sequoia into the deal, drove the company to think bigger—but not so much by a specific action or a single suggestion. It came more from his repeated urgings.

"He really added value by trying to set the bar higher for the company, for what the company could do," says Stolle, "by pushing me, pushing management to be more strategic, more important, more critical to our customers. Just by asking the right questions: 'You're solving an important problem, but how do you become fundamental, core to the company's business?'"

No matter how they're conveyed, formally or informally, structured or on the fly, value-added services come at a price. Founders and entrepreneurs give up a portion of their companies for the hands-on assistance. One of the reason the system works that way is because often equity is all most start-ups can offer. And it gives the investors powerful incentive to provide their services tirelessly, to make sure their equity will eventually be worth something. "We get paid nothing but equity. We invest alongside you, and if things go south, they go south for us too," points out Mike Linnert, the partner at Technology Crossover Ventures.

Entrepreneurs could get most of the same services elsewhere. Even if they don't have the cash or the credit to bring in big-league consulting outfits, some professional service providers also take equity as payment. In *High Stakes, No Prisoners*, Charles Ferguson reports that when he set up Vermeer Technologies, he gave away private stock like candy, paying attorneys and business consultants that way because, before Vermeer attracted VC funding, it was too strapped to offer cash. He passed out so many shares that when his venture investors arrived, they coerced him to wrestle some of it back. But unlike venture capitalists, consultants taking equity as payment basically take it on faith—or hope—that their client will succeed and its stock value will appreciate. Sure, they provide their specialty service. But that's all they can provide. On the other hand, successful VCs assist a start-up across a wide spectrum of business services, and they tinker tirelessly with the workings of the company in most ways conceivable.

But that advantage is a bit harder to claim in cases where venture capital moves into dotcom partnerships with Fortune 1000 companies, like the Wal-Mart deal penned between the mammoth retailer and Accel Partners. Clearly Wal-Mart can afford to hire all the consulting help its executives ever fancy.

"I've heard the response that we don't add the value we charge for," says Michael Linnert. The charge gets made as his firm, Technology Crossover Ventures, tries to set itself up as a specialist in handling spin-offs and partnerships with pre-Internet companies. For one, it brought Ace Hardware into an alliance with its portfolio holding OurHouse.com. "Someone can say, 'Well, I can get all those things best-of-breed from someone else. I could go to Heidrick & Struggles and get recruiting a lot cheaper than I get it from you. I could then go to McKinsey and get strategy help for a lot cheaper than I get it from you. I could then go and hire a great business development guy, and get that kind of help a lot cheaper than I get it from you. I could stitch together all those things you bring to the table and then I could put together an advisory board of Internet companies and bring to bear some of their experience on the Internet.' And the question that people then ask is, 'So given all that, how do I justify giving you 20 percent of the company, when I could probably spend the equivalent of three percent of the company to get all that stuff, including raising the cash?' We find that skepticism coming a lot more fast and furiously as we start talking to the Fortune 1000 companies about how we can help them move onto the Internet."

One reply to the skeptics is that Internet companies operate outside of the experience of traditional commerce. They operate according to a new dynamic called increasing returns, whereby the company that moves the fastest and therefore grows the biggest builds up the momentum it needs to grow bigger still at the expense of everyone else. It's like a snowball rolling downhill. Or like Amazon, starting out as a bookseller and then adding music and toys and whatever else it discovers it can sell. The corporation's returns increase because, according to at least one theory, the gangly Goliath getting all the customers has more chances to probe and play and experiment in order to learn what the customers want, which enables it to bring in even more customers.

"If you believe that, then the reward for being number one is always going to be disproportionately larger than the reward for being number two or three," Linnert explains. "By the time you get down to number[s] four and five, you probably won't even exist." Therefore, he says, "the key is to do everything you can to be number one. And it all revolves around speed. The biggest challenge is making the jump to light speed to compete on the Internet. Once you've made a decision, you can't have McKinsey come in and spend six months honing it. You've got to start running. So a venture capitalist can come to Wal-Mart or to a Wal-Mart competitor or to whoever else might be moving onto the Internet and say, 'Hey, we can increase the chances pretty significantly that you're number one, because we do all those things in parallel. We do them fast and furiously, and arguably we actually do recruit better than, you know, Heidrick & Struggles. We may provide better consulting help than McKinsey, because we're specialized. And if we can help increase your chances of being number one, then you're actually better served to take us. Because you're better off owning 80 percent of something that's disproportionately large, than owning 99 percent of something that's the second place player, from whom the reward is disproportionately small.'"

Involvement and participation in the companies they invest in is key to top-shelf VCs, and it should prove fundamental to the companies they service. It boils down to the fact that the venture people possess specialized experience that comes from exposure to new business structures—in this case, the Internet. New business, after all, is the realm in which venture capital operates.

7

BIG PICTURE KNOWLEDGE

Fresh out of college in 1975, an electrical engineering degree from Iowa State University in hand, serious-minded, hardworking, ambitious, creative, exacting, analytical, and very dedicated Nancy Schoendorf went to work in the manufacturing operations of Hewlett-Packard. One of the first things she learned is that manufacturing is all screwed up. Not that Hewlett-Packard is worse than anyone else. In fact, given its historical position as one of the preeminent computer and electronics makers, HP probably does better than most. But manufacturing by its nature is a difficult exercise. Behind all the big, rumbling machines, the chattering gears, roaring blowers, recirculating belts, and other, assorted whirring gizmos, the difficulty that trips up manufacturing operations the most is the coordination of information. Manufacturing runs on information—plus a couple cans of lubricant and a box of spare fuses. There are product plans, parts lists, production schedules, supplier IDs, inventory accounts, ship dates, status reports, work orders, engineering changes, and on and on. Most every piece of information about a product relates in one way or another to every other information bit regarding that product. The data originates from many scattered sources. It heads in many different directions, to different people doing different jobs. Most of it is time-sensitive. A lot of it is urgent. Some of it is outright mission critical, exerting a sizable influence on the manufacturer's costs, on its profit margins, and therefore on its bottom line. But as important as all that data may be, juggling it requires so much skill, dexterity, and coordination that sometimes it's a wonder that factories work at all.

Nancy Schoendorf witnessed the confusion during her first stint out of college. Her first assignment for Hewlett-Packard was to move product plans from engineering to production, a job that made all those intractable data-communication headaches become her headaches. She didn't forget them even after she had left the job far behind. Therefore, as a general partner with Mohr Davidow Ventures, when Schoendorf first connected with Bryan Stolle of Agile Software in 1995—when Agile, in Stolle's words, was only "three smiley faces and a business plan"—she jumped at his idea for software that smoothes out the information path between the designers who create things on paper and the manufacturers who must ultimately make sense of the plans and the production orders.

"I understood the business problem," she attests. "I was a person who would have used the product Bryan was describing. So I had a very good sense in my gut of what it was, and what it could be."

Schoendorf cautions that such first-person, practical familiarity with an entrepreneur's product or concept or new business approach remains a rarity for a venture capitalist. After all, private experience can expose a person to only so much. But it can get you much nearer to the goal: to operate with such in-depth, intimate knowledge about a market, a business sector, or a technology that you know its present position and you can predict its trajectory. This insider's intimacy helps VCs make better, go/no-go investment decisions, and make them faster. Once inside a company, it forms the foundation of the value-add they apply to help assure the investment's success.

Venture capitalists today are specialists. Each restricts his or her investments to limited and defined interests, where he or she has acquired enough expertise to see the big picture in all its depth and detail. They want to foresee its approaching, unfulfilled needs so that they can accurately assess the odds of success for any business plan that takes a fresh crack at satisfying them. Also, VCs want to know a field well enough to recognize when it is already saturated with competitors, so they can avoid me-too investments. After all, the biggest returns often come from companies that get to a market first, and develop it without the distraction of dogfights with rivals.

"You recognize an opportunity faster because you don't need to do a lot of research," says John Fisher. "You understand it intuitively right away, because you know your market, so you can respond more quickly, beat the competition and scoop the deal." The advantage shows in Don Valentine's account of Sequoia's original investment in Cisco in the 1980s. Other venture firms had said no to the entrepreneurs, but Sequoia recognized the company's potential, because it had learned the language while making earlier investments in networking gear. Eager to play, it put together a deal that helped it mitigate its management misgivings.

After an investment is made, much of the value-add a VC brings to a portfolio company comes out of what he knows about an industry. Like whom to meet, which customers to angle for, what acquisitions to pursue, and so on. "In some cases, we know our market better than the entrepreneurs do," Fisher explains, echoing a view that's heard commonly on the venture circuit. After all, a VC churns through a lot of new business plans that slant toward his specialty, giving him insight into a lot of distant corners of the field. Through other investments within a specialty, he has a sense of its historic development. He knows the movers. The shakers, too. "Sometimes we end up telling them, 'You're on to something here, but you don't have it quite right. Make a change in this direction with this business model and I'll fund you.' And the entrepreneur says, 'Ah-ha. You're right. Beautiful.'"

The expertise gets specialized and exclusive, giving VCs an insider's advantage but locking them out of deals beyond their fields. It's the same for a real estate developer who's an old hand at commercial buildings but who might be only dimly aware of the tricks and trade-offs on the residential side of the business. Sure, the structures go up according to the same engineering principles. But a home builder doesn't know a single elevator contractor. And an office-park developer couldn't guess which realtor would be best to represent his subdivision.

In the public equity markets, stock is stock, and the buying and selling of it proceeds pretty much the same no matter what the issue, by no matter which company. The secret, of course, is determining which companies' equity to purchase, and which to avoid. That's where more than a passing acquaintance with a particular industry can help an investor forecast either sunny days or looming storm clouds for an intended stock. Does the future of William Clay Ford, Jr.'s, company look brighter after it paid about $2.7 billion to purchase Land Rover from Bavarian Motor Works in 2000? A superficial analysis might hold that only good things could come of it. After all, Rover is the premier name in sport-utility vehicles. It makes the hoity-toity, high-priced flagships of the entire vehicle class, and as a class, SUVs are the hottest vehicles carmakers have going right now. But Ford already holds the dominant position in SUV sales volume. Can it sell Land Rovers without cannibalizing some of its own highfliers? And how might the acquisition play in an auto-sales downturn? After all, Rover has been a bit of a financial millstone of late, unable to make any money. And even if Ford can clean up the British brand's balance sheet, might demand for SUVs cool if fuel prices reach the pain-in-the-tank threshold they seemed to be approaching when Ford made the purchase in mid-2000? And what about government regulations? Looming EPA crackdowns on these big, fuel-thirsty trucks could make them a lot less desirable to the day-care-tripping moms who buy them up like motorized candy. Unless an investor followed the car business pretty closely, he probably wouldn't even know that the government scolds were beginning to grumble about trucks.

In venture investing, you'll hear terms like "domain expertise," "sector knowledge," and "vertical market insight." Basically, they mean knowing a business inside and out. Knowing its technological foundation. Its competitive landscape. Its influential buyers. Its combative sellers. Its historical development. Its likely direction.

"I don't know how the steel industry works. I do know how the Internet industry works," says J. Neil Weintraut of 21st Century Internet Capital Partners. Of course, there's some danger in acquiring a specific and sometimes narrow specialization. Ask Izhar Armony what happens if his field of focus, business-to-business Internet systems, stops paying returns. "I'm toast," he shoots back in acquired English still tinged with the accent of his homeland on the sunny east Mediterranean. Other partners at Charles River Ventures, investing in business segments that remained in favor, would carry Charles River, he explains. In the meantime, Armony would get busy acquiring knowledge and expertise in another segment.

For a lot of venture capitalists, the knowledge starts with her professional, pre-VC background and experience, as it did for Nancy Schoendorf. Tom Dyal, a founding partner of the Sand Hill firm Redpoint Ventures, learned about communications equipment first as an engineer and manager at AT&T Bell Labs (which became Lucent Technologies), and then as a product manager at Bay Networks. He followed the technical track even as a student. Dyal's master's degree, from Stanford University, is in electrical engineering. Ann Winblad of Hummer Winblad Venture Partners started and ran her own software company before she cofounded the venture firm, which specializes in making software investments.

Of course, software itself is a very broad field, so any investor focused there still has a lot of space to wander about. One of the tricks to VC specialization is to not get too narrowly channeled. Market niches can get awfully crowded. Once one fills up, there's much less room to maneuver new investments. Besides, if your expertise is too restricted, it won't help you assess a promising portfolio opportunity in a niche next door.

"I focus on communications," explains Redpoint's Dyal, "so I'm looking at everything from communications silicon [microchips] to communication equipment, to Internet infrastructure to services. All of those are fairly related. The chip companies sell to the equip-

ment companies. The equipment companies sell to the service companies. And there's a lot of the same trends that happen across all
those industries. Take the roll-out of DSL [digital subscriber loop]
and cable modems, the roll-out of optical networks. Well, guess
what? When you start looking at them, the roll-outs of these new
technologies are not that different from what happened in the previous generation."

Thus Hummer Winblad's software focus still lets it into a diversity of action. Its investments swing from the company MyDru-
gRep, a Web place for health care workers to find pharmaceutical
info, to Napster, the Internet music-sharing service beloved by college dorm-dwellers but so reviled by recording companies that they
sued to shut it down. (In a telling example of VC involvement,
Hummer Winblad was involved in the company's legal defense.)
And those are just in the Internet software category. Hummer's con-
sumer-software buy-ins include Books That Work, a publisher of
electronic lifestyle guides for adults, and Humongous Entertain-
ment, interactive software for tots. After that there are still other
categories, like enterprise software, software development tools,
desktop systems, and scientific and engineering systems, all within
the firm's field of focus.

Some venture firms still maintain more diversified portfolios that
span across the high-tech spectrum, though typically the individual
partners within these wider-ranging firms specialize. Outside of Silicon Valley, business conditions can both require and permit a
broader approach. At Advantage Capital down in New Orleans,
Steven Stull isn't forced to funnel the firm into a narrow specialization, because Advantage doesn't need the deep sector knowledge
necessary to stay ahead of fierce competition for deals. On the
other hand, Advantage doesn't see a concentration of deals in a single sector that would allow it to narrowly specialize. "If there were
two hundred VC firms here, there would certainly be a competitive
advantage to having your own niche," Stull says. "But being one of
the few, if not only source of capital in the area, we see transactions
across a wide range of industries." It's not likely a Sand Hill VC

will see a business plan promoting a new oil exploration technology. But in Advantage's neighborhood down by the Gulf, "we see a lot of opportunities in that area, and we've invested in a few of them."

Overall, across-the-board specialization by an entire firm has grown a lot more common since the sea-change technology called the Internet arrived with so many rich opportunities. Some venture firms have acquired an I-net focus more or less by default, with Internet-related investments automatically taking over their portfolios only because so many promising Web deals appeared. Although Draper Fisher Jurvetson formally began life with a broader focus, it's gone 100 percent Internet since it started doling out its DFJ IV fund in 1997. Charles River divides its practice into two specialties, e-commerce and communication equipment. But in both cases, says Rick Burnes, "probably 85 percent of what we've done in the last five years has been Internet related." That includes software to run on the Internet, software used to run the Internet, and networking and communications hardware that, in physical terms, equals the Internet. "The Internet is as broad as box companies [networking gear] like Lucent, all the way to a gift company" that runs a Web site selling hearts and flowers, he says.

Some later-coming VC practices arrived on account of the Web. Redpoint formed in autumn 1999 with the sole mission of funding Internet start-ups. The six venturers who created it had left the more diversified, well-established Silicon Valley firms Brentwood Venture Capital and Institutional Venture Partners (IVP). Those firms still carry on investment activities in medical devices, biotechnology, semiconductors, and the like. But the defectors teamed together as Redpoint because they espied opportunities for a sharply focused Internet specialist. 21st Century Internet Venture Partners was spun out of Hummer Winblad in late 1996. Its focus is obvious. Less obvious—at least from its name alone—is its aim to change the world. 21st Century Internet calls itself "a venture firm for the new economy," explaining in the mission statement that pops up on its Web site that "new economy companies are companies that are incarnating a new digital—but most significantly better—world by innovating markets, value propositions and technology itself."

That's not all huff and wind, by the way. Henry McCance of Greylock ticks off "new economy" as a term already well integrated into his professional vocabulary. McCance in no faddist, though he's certainly witnessed a lot of fads soar, fizzle, and crash. Henry McCance has probably personally logged more venture-investing years than the combined years-in-service of every member of 21st Century Internet Venture Partners, from its two general partners down to its receptionist. Yet McCance retains a youthful appreciation for the adventure and even the mystery of new-business formation, and when he speaks about the new economy, he means the same thing as the upstarts: It's a historical discontinuity.

"I believe that 50 years from now or 100 years from now, when historians are looking back, they will look at this period as being much more important than the industrial revolution," the veteran predicts. "And that's not hyperbole. That's what I believe. You just have to think about trivial examples. I have a daughter who keeps in touch daily with her 40 closest friends. They live all over the globe, but it's just second nature to her. That's just a trivial example. It's not going to change the world, but it's changing her life."

When McCance joined Greylock in 1969, he entered an arcane and little-known profession that demanded a lot less domain expertise. The business of boosting young companies wasn't organized around a particular industry. Instead, it demanded tireless determination to learn anew about the market circumstances surrounding a target investment. Back then, due diligence meant researching an entire industry as well as learning the particulars about the company that caught your eye. The few institutional venture capitalists in practice were generalists, investing in any young company that showed promise, no matter its business. The young Greylock still made its greatest concentration of investments in the technologies of the era, but it also had room to venture a lot more intrepidly than any firm would dare today. In 1966, when it was still only an infant, Greylock bought into a wig company, Reid-Meredith. Fore-shadowing necessities to come, the investment fizzled largely as a consequence of Greylock's lack of experience in the field—lack of domain expertise in lady's high-fashion headdresses. "We did not realize that we were buying in at the top of the market," writes Bill Elfers in his book *Greylock*. "Customers and market checks told the investors where the company was, but not accurately where it was going." The lesson the firm took from the experience: "The risk of failure is substantially increased when you are inexperienced in the field."

The lesson still applies, though it's not likely you'll see a contemporary VC investing in a wig maker (though an investment in an Internet wig retailer isn't outside the question). Changes brought about by the growth of the business have by now vanquished generalist venture capital. "If someone came to me with a biotechnology company, I wouldn't touch it," illustrates Fisher. "If someone came with a medical-device concept: wouldn't touch it. We deal in stuff that we understand."

Nowadays, due diligence has to be more or less completed before a VC even sees a proposal. He may still have time to shake down the management team, running a quick credit check and phoning references. But the fundamental value of the concept—its ability to satisfy legitimate customer needs, its competitive position within its business segment, the time horizon before it's likely to be eclipsed—should appear clear as day to the venture capitalists the first time he scans the business plan. If the concept has value, and he misses it on the first pass, someone else is likely to catch it before he has time to scratch his head and wonder.

"We have made investment decisions in four hours," says Izhar Armony. "If you see a good deal, that's a competitive deal, and you need to take time to do due diligence, you won't get there. Market knowledge is extremely important, to be able to make informed decisions fast."

The cutthroat competition is a payback for the industry's conspicuous success. And it's not just competition to beat the rivals to a good deal. Because of the frenetic pace of high-tech business cre-ation—with VCs encouraging more entrepreneur-technologists to give it a go, and more entrepreneur-technologists clamoring for chunks of the action—venture capitalists find it harder to establish portfolio winners before competing companies with related ideas come out of the unknown to capture the new markets themselves, or at least to contend for them.

"You start by understanding the dynamics of your sectors," says Ann Winblad. For one thing, that can prevent a VC from getting caught backing a technology or concept that's soon going to be made obsolete by a better idea from competitor X. Jim Hynes, the former Fidelity venture chief, opines: "If you're not following what's going on, you can say, 'that looks like the greatest thing in the world.' But there might be something being worked on over here that's going to leap-frog it. For every 10,000 ideas you see or hear, one is good. I can't tell you how much garbage pours over the desk."

"You have to sort of recognize the warm spots," says Winblad, "'cause if they are hot spots, it's too late. Before, you had time to say, okay, I think I see something warming up. I see two sticks be-ing rubbed together. Let's fund the cub scouts and build a troop. We had a lot more time. Now, you go to the campground and there are thousands of little cub scouts going . . . " (she completes the analogy by hunching forward and rapidly miming the frantic, fire-by-two-sticks method).

But specialization is more than just a defensive maneuver. It also leads VCs to significant discoveries. Draper Fisher Jurvetson's in-sider expertise in data-communication services led it to the Web when it placed its first Internet investment in late 1993—an early date that, according to Fisher's suspicion, makes it "the first Inter-net investment of any of the Silicon Valley venture-capital firms." The fact is, however, many of the high-flying Valley firms claim to be I-way pioneers as well.

The firm started life in 1985 under Timothy Draper, with John Fisher and Steve Jurvetson signing on in increments. In the late

1980s, it specialized in communications. That focus introduced it to the on-line service companies emerging in the late eighties and early nineties. On-line services were precursors to the universal Internet: They united computer users over the public phone system, but you had to subscribe to the service to play, and your participation was limited to that service alone. They were more like privately operated turnpikes, less like universally accessible interstate freeways. Draper Fisher lost money on its first outing, "but these were businesses that we loved, and we knew they were going to change the way people do things," Fisher recounts.

The partners gained valuable insight into the nature of on-line communications. For one thing, says Fisher, they recognized the early systems' shortcomings. "It was just too darn clumsy for people to install software and dial up private network connections. There wasn't a browser." Therefore, when Web browsers appeared as accommodating gateways allowing personal computers to enter a ubiquitous data and communications network, the firm leaped at the opportunities the development presented. "It was just this breakthrough: a standard, low-cost platform that everybody could have access to."

As a consequence of its quick pickup, Fisher says, "in early 97 we were 100 percent focused on the Internet at the same time that most of the venture capital firms were still only sticking their toes into the water." Even though its first bona fide Internet investment returned only "a modest multiple," the direction was clearly established. Two-thirds of Draper's 1995 fund went into Internet companies. By the time it ventured out to invest DFJ IV, its 1997 fund, the company backed Internet concerns exclusively. The consequence: In March 2000, three years after that fund closed, its portfolio had seen ten IPOs, five acquisitions, one write-off, and four investments still to be resolved. The fund's $97 million went to twenty start-ups, which had returned more than $3 billion by March 2000, according to Fisher.

But market knowledge does more than lead VCs to high-return, green-field concepts first. It also helps them land the better deals when they arrive. The best entreps—the ones with the business-building personalities that every VC hunts for—expect their venture partners to bring the value-added experience, insight, contacts, and connections that can only come from intimate participation in a business field.

"The power has shifted to the entrepreneurs," observes Armony. "They can take money from a hundred different players. They will work with people that they respect, and people that can add value. Part of that value will be, do I understand your industry? Do I have lots of customer contacts? Do I have other people that you can hire into the company? That's all market knowledge."

"You're a much more attractive investor for an entrepreneur if you understand his market," Fisher notes. "You can add a lot more value if you have connections in the marketplace. You are much more likely to make them more successful."

The whole object of value-added services is to make the entrepreneurial venture more successful, and business knowledge provides the foundation of value-add.

When very young companies led by first-time entrepreneurs are involved, venture capitalists must also employ expertise that's more fundamental than industry-specific domain knowledge. Call it management and operational expertise. The organizational niceties are what a new company needs to adopt as it grows from a few frantic founders operating out of the CEO's rec room to a bona fide business with employees and equipment, offices, and maybe even an actual product to sell. For all the scorn he heaps on his venture investors, Charles Ferguson expresses gratitude at least for their organizational and administrative expertise in his book *High Stakes, No Prisoners*. After closing Vermeer's first round, writes the one-time entrepreneur, "the VCs and their lawyers took me to school on the capital structure of start-ups. In general, I give them high marks on this score. For the most part, they explained things clearly and honestly—in fact, I learned much more from them than from our own lawyers—and they treated me fairly." He describes how the small-biz specialists excoriated him for having passed out too many company shares.

"You need to be consistent in your practices, but an entrepreneur whose company has already been up and running for four and five months may have had no advice like that," points out Weintraut of 21st Century Internet Capital. "Say you hire one engineer in the heat of the moment and you give that engineer 15,000 shares. The next day you hire another at the same grade and you give him 10,000. How long do you think it is going to take for those two to talk? Before long, you have one pissed off engineer, 'cause he says my peer has more options than I do. And before you know it, you could wind up with a discombobulated equity structure where there is not enough equity left to attract your VPs. But if somebody like me comes in and says, 'Well, you know what, I've seen this problem in 10 different companies,' I can prevent the company from giving away too much stock on a helter skelter basis. We can create a stock-option budget. We can prevent a company from having a lot of employment issues."

This is a return to the VC's traditional role of helping to turn aspiring companies into real companies that are built on common business practices. Together with segment expertise, the knowledge can help VCs counsel portfolio companies to avoid blunders. Early in its life, the Web start-up GoTo had decided to farm out the development of critical software that would lay the foundation for its business. GoTo is an Internet directory—an index, or maybe a table of contents—that sends consumers who are looking for specific merchandise to Web sites that sell it. Tell it to search for, say, "briefcase," and GoTo returns with links to eBags, Luggage Online, Irv's Luggage Warehouse, and dozens of others. Each listing site pays for each visitor that finds it through GoTo. But each listing site sets its own price it will pay per visitor. The location that pays the most gets listed first, with each listing after it ranked according to its per-hit payment. That sets up competitive bidding whereby commercial Web sites increase the amount they'll pay per hit in order to move up above competitors in the GoTo listing. The software the company sought to farm out ranks the list, changing the order instantaneously when a Web site gets eager enough for more business that it bids up its payment.

Exercising the principle of investor involvement, Draper Fisher Jurvetson objected to GoTo's plan to outsource the software's development. The firm acted from a combination of flat-out business-management experience and some domain expertise related to Web-system development. Experience had taught the venture partners that outsourced software typically takes twice as long to develop than the contractor promised, and costs two to three times as much as originally quoted. Besides that, says Fisher, "outsourcing the key components to your ultimate success is always a mistake. We had a huge row with the founders over this. We prevailed. They hired a team internally and they built it on time and on budget and went public on time. They only did it because they trusted us. We've seen the movie a thousand times before and they haven't."

For the most, part industry-segment knowledge comes as on-the-job training. Armony joined Charles River in 1997 after working as an associate for General Atlantic Partners. While there he got a good look at what's called "enterprise applications"—the software that corporations use to help manage their business operations—but when he made it his specialty at Charles River, he says, "I had to start from scratch. Not too much reading. More interacting with people—people who are successful in the marketplace. You go out, buy them lunch, buy them dinner. And also, your investments tend to cross-fertilize each other. You're doing number one; number two in a similar sector is different, but there are similarities."

That's not to say there's never any critical study and analysis. While he was still conducting his critical analysis of the Crosspoint portfolio in 1994, Seth Neiman was also educating himself on the intricacies of the computer memory market. Leading him there was a prospective deal that kind of danced around a difficulty that powerful computers were having communicating with storage systems.

"A project surfaced that identified this problem peripherally and proposed a business that was kind of loosely about fixing the problem," he recounts. "It wasn't a very good business. It didn't have the right technology. It didn't have the right people. But it sort of made me aware of the problem." At issue was the fact that the big, networked enterprise applications taking off at the time needed a better connection to get data out of a company's information inventory. "A networking model needed to be applied to the way computers access storage," Neiman explains.

The technical issues were virgin territory for him. He took six months studying the problem, reading trade journals, visiting computer suppliers, making rounds with a consultant he hired to guide him into the territory. Through the process he built enough conviction to recommend an investment even though, at the time, he was only "loosely coupled," as he says, with Crosspoint. He ended up exercising true-blue VC involvement, incubating Brocade Communication Systems in 1995—starting the company from scratch rather than picking up an entrepreneur's creation. He served as its first chief executive officer. As of this writing, the company continues to roll up momentum. Stock buyers valued it at $65 million when it went public in May 1999. For the 2000 fiscal year, its $69 million in revenues represented 180 percent growth in sales. It boasts of more than 80 percent share of the market for networking devices connecting servers to data storage systems.

Not a bad start for Neiman. But only a start. As a venture capitalist focuses assiduously on a single market or sector, knowledge and understanding grow cumulatively. Neither Jim Swartz of Accel Partners nor Bandel Carano of Oak Investment Partners could have predicted that the early lessons they learned investing in videophones would replay at Polycom. Oak is an Accel neighbor, with an office on University Avenue in Palo Alto, as well as in Westport, Connecticut, and Minneapolis. Together in July 1991, Accel and Oak backed Brian Hinman seven months after the entrepreneur started Polycom. Hinman had been one of the founders of PictureTel, an original, now-you-see-'em videophone maker. In fact, Swartz met Hinman in 1988 when the VC-led investor group restructured PictureTel. At Polycom, as the lead investors for their firms, Swartz and Carano took seats on the board of directors.

At Polycom, Hinman set out to develop and sell tabletop conference-room telephones. Its triangular, UFO-modeled squawk boxes today still dominate the market they largely created, although first the product had to clear some formidable design and distribution hurdles. No sooner was it on track when Polycom launched into videophones in 1994. The suggestion for that business-growing departure came first from Carano, with both Hinman and Swartz following rapidly with approval. Just the same, the plan looked like a Quixotic adventure that pitted Polycom against the then-formidable PictureTel. But, says Swartz, "all three of us knew enough about the video business, having been involved at PictureTel and other companies, to see the opportunity way ahead of its time and act on it." The result: Polycom seized market leadership from PictureTel. The product extension, says Swartz, accounts for "a couple-hundred-million-dollar business." And the company keeps going. In May 2000, Polycom broke through with a $600 personal videophone. Called ViaVideo, it plugs into personal computers and carries live video conversations over the Internet. That joins Polycom's original ViewStation line of group videophones for conference rooms, which start at $4,000. "This is what it's all about," beams Swartz. "We built a real company. We had lots of problems, but we built enormous value."

For a VC like Swartz, with sage experience acquired through twenty-eight years at the undertaking (he started in the profession in 1972, and founded Accel in 1984), questions of knowledge, know-how, and business savvy don't come up. But a lot of younger bloods have to sell their experience and expertise more eagerly. In the competition for top-shelf entrepreneurs, the possession of live, pre-VC experience sets up a kind of divide between venture practitioners who have it and those who don't. Some come with technical backgrounds, who actually made products and sold them. Others took a professional turn as an entrepreneur. Still others worked as corporate executives and managers before they became VCs. There are some who did all the above. In every case, they sell that experience against competing investors who came to the trade most often from the financial professions, like the many securities analysts and banking men who jumped into private-equity investing.

"We are really quite different from most of the venture business," says Seth Neiman of Crosspoint Venture Partners, illustrating the divide. "We are all people with long operating backgrounds: not HR or legal, but line managers and executives, running a business, building products. So it makes us think about things a little bit differently." Neiman himself worked as vice president of product development for an outfit called Dahlgren Control Systems. He graduated to a similar role for a subsidiary of Sun Microsystems before he founded his own company, Coactive Computing.

When Greylock went on a hiring spree in 1999, adding partners to fill up its California office, the firm shopped carefully for former entrepreneurs who would turn the heads of aspiring business chiefs.

"We wanted people with technical undergraduate degrees. We're investing in technology, and you need to talk the talk and walk the walk," McCance explains. "We wanted them to have an MBA, because to a certain degree, schools like the Stanford Business School and the Harvard Business School are just so hard to get into. They put a filter on excellence. We wanted them to have good business and operating experience. And then, most importantly, we wanted people who worked in the kinds of companies that we want to back, and to have enjoyed huge success in that entrepreneurial experience."

Why? "If the entrepreneur has the choice of all these people to give him the capital and to be on his board, he is going to look and say, gee, this individual has faced the exact same challenges and decisions that I'm about the face. And he's done it recently. He understands what I'm going to do, and he succeeded. That would be a great background to have as a partner. And he knows that it's not going to go straight up. He's going to have some patience with me."

The firm found Aneel Bhusri, who moved into the Palo Alto office in 1999, and who was senior vice president in charge of product strategy, business development, and marketing at Peoplesoft, a noted maker of enterprise software. He still sits as Peoplesoft vice chairman. Charles Chi became a Greylock general partner in 2000, moving over from Ciena, where he was vice president of marketing.

Before that, Chi cofounded Lightera Networks, a maker of optical switches for telecommunications that was acquired by Ciena. Ciena, a highly regarded manufacturer of optical networking equipment, is itself an entrepreneurial success story. Started in 1992, the company closed its first venture-financing round in 1994, with backing from Sevin Rosen Funds, InterWest Partners, and Vanguard Venture Partners. A second round at the tail end of 1994 brought Charles River into the fold. Finally, in late 1995, Weiss Peck & Greer led Ciena's third round. In all, the company took in about $40 million in private equity before its IPO in 1997.

Lastly, David Sze joined Greylock just after Chi. Before enlisting in venture capital, he was senior vice president for the Web company Excite@Home, where he handled product strategy.

"I couldn't get a job at Greylock today, with the background that I had when I joined the firm," shoots McCance. "I joined as raw material. A good academic record, maybe. But no operating experience. The founders of Greylock taught me the business. I was the apprentice to three great craftsmen." In addition to William Elfers, they were Dan Gregory and Charlie Waite. Generalists all.

No matter how it's acquired, information and understanding do not insulate venture players from mistakes. In fact, at times knowledge and experience can even mislead. Sequoia Capital originally passed on Agile Software partly because, years earlier, Sequoia had suffered through an investment gone bad in Sherpa Systems, Bryan Stolle's alma mater. Though Stolle's proposal for Agile represented a significant diversion from Sherpa, its software is still classified as what's called product data management, the same as Sherpa. The field had never quite taken off.

"That clearly was a specter," says Michael Moritz, the Sequoia partner who eventually brought the firm to Agile as a second-round investor. "We had been an investor in a company in the product data management business, and that made us somewhat wary. The company had struggled. It had not been successful. The investment had been very disappointing, so why go and invest again in an arena [that] had been very disappointing?"

After Mohr Davidow made a first-round plunge, getting Agile a boost off the ground at least, Moritz took a second look. "One of the things about the venture business is that occasionally you have the opportunity to fess up to a mistake. We may be wrong once, we try not to make the same mistake twice. So Bryan very kindly and thoughtfully came back, and we saw the light."

And, of course, an insider's knowledge won't always cinch the deal, either. For all its vaunted Internet expertise, Draper Fisher Jurvetson couldn't snare Yahoo. Fisher says his firm was the first venture capital outfit that Yahoo founders Jerry Yang and David Filo called on. That was April 1995. Cofounder Tim Draper offered the pair $250,000 for a 25 percent share. They turned him down, and two months later they gave the quarter share to Sequoia for a $1 million investment. Draper Fisher Jurvetson would have put up as much, but at the time, says Fisher, "we had a small fund and we just didn't have the money. Tim was shattered. He wanted that deal so badly, he was absolutely shattered."

8

STEELY DETERMINATION

In the Internet age it became hard to practice persistence in venture capital. Things happened so fast. For a while at least, there scarcely was time, or the need, to ride with an investment through long runs of frustrations, surprises, setbacks, turnarounds, miscalculations, calamities, and recoveries. Therefore, rather than talk much about the determination to sweat through downturns, or discuss the resolution to battle protracted competitive incursions, or extol the courage to stand by untested product concepts, many VCs instead expounded at length about first-mover advantage. That means getting to a market first, so you have room to run around and play before any competitor starts clamoring for your customers' attention. How often can the example be repeated? Amazon got there first, and after Amazon there is no point in anyone else trying to sell books on-line.

Some venture veterans even speculated that as an investment principle, persistence had grown obsolete. The days of about-faces, second chances, and epic reversals are gone, the argument goes. Today you get it right the first time, or someone else will.

But venture capital is all about change, and a good venture capitalist realizes that he can even change the rules to subvert mighty Amazon, the icon among Web brands. Besides, Amazon probably didn't even arrive first to its market. Odds are very good that other Web-based booksellers appeared before Jeff Bezos's juggernaut, and some cyber-historian will one day enjoy the challenge of uncovering their accounts in a musty Internet archive. But no matter who moved first, clearly Amazon moved better than every other predecessor and contemporary—or at least it moved adroitly enough to vanquish its rivals. Still, to an ordinary VC, first-mover advantage means only getting to a market first. To the savvy VC, first-mover advantage means getting to a concept first. After all, a brilliant concept can conquer a market, no matter who owns it. There's no reason to doubt that someone with a brighter idea will someday sell books to Amazon's readers.

But in 1997 and 98 and 99, conventional thinkers took first-mover advantage only to mean that they could win by backing the first Web-based furniture store, or on-line health-food shop, or pet-supply seller, or women's athletic-wear retailer, or shoe salesman, wine club, garden-hose hawker, pincushion specialist. For a while it looked like they were right, as long as Nasdaq's wild enthusiasm for Web stocks lasted. But as the market for new companies moved into the new century, a lot of these first movers were already moving out. "People have just been killed in retail," Rick Burnes observed of the carnage. So much for conventional thinking.

Likewise with persistence. Discerning VCs recognized that after the generous market aberration passed, success in venture capital would once again require stick-to-it tenacity.

"It's just been masked by the strong capital market," says Bill Kaiser of Greylock. "When it looks like persistence doesn't matter anymore, I think it's just because the capital markets have made everybody look smarter than they really are."

Successful VCs win the race by staying in it. That may require little more than stubbornness. It's an inbred adherence to that old adage "If at first you don't succeed. . . ." Thus, determination appears to be a personal attribute that the best venture capitalists are born with. It's probably attached to their pride and their striving after achievement. Certainly it's a part of their competitiveness.

Nancy Schoendorf sums it up when she confides, "I don't like to lose. I don't like to lose at all."

That's her best explanation for why she stuck improbably to an investment gone bad until it turned good. In fact, she expects Mohr Davidow to end up netting a handsome sum on the adventure. But she still seems surprised and a bit chagrined that she stood by the company through so much. "If there was ever a deal that I should not have invested in," she says, "this is it. If I knew, from the work I put in, that I was going to get this outcome, yeah, I'd do it again. But I think the odds of having worked our way through these rapids to end up with a great company are so small that I would never take that risk again.

"I changed out the entire development team. I changed out the management team—more than once. I had a meeting in this very room with the chief technology officer, who was the family jewels. He basically said, 'Either you fire the CEO or I'm quitting. And you'd better do it by tomorrow.' There were so many times when I thought that this was not going to make it. But with persistence in finding the right people to bring into the company, it is, I think, going to be a terrific investment for us."

It's not so much that she picked wrong when she decided to back the company, which she won't name. Schoendorf confesses that she suffered some queasiness from the start about the original management. But, she says, "there was something about it that made me want to do the deal."

She stuck with it because instead of simply shrugging her shoulders, she always looked resolutely for a reason to hold on. "Whenever you thought, well, they can't get through this, there was some glimmer," she recollects. "At various times it was different things. In a lot of cases it was in the product. And in a lot of cases it was the market. And sometimes, depending on which rapid we were going through at the time, it was an individual we hired who made you say, 'I think this guy can get us through it.' It was never hopeless," she says. "It required a tradeoff of working a little bit harder."

Hanging on tightly to a new venture follows from a different rationale than the commonplace rule that admonishes consumers and some more conventional investors to hold on to stocks, fund shares, and other paper for the long haul. For one thing, compounding isn't an element of venture capital, at least not the way compounding works in personal investment portfolios. A VC increases the value of an investment by helping to create a useful new entity. That's a lot different from accumulating wealth by letting returns pile on top of each other over time. For another, in stable and legitimate democracies—where corporations and other private property are safe from rapacious government—history shows that stock-market holdings increase in value over time, despite the inevitable dips and backslides that economists call recessions and depressions. Invest in the New York Stock Exchange and you'll certainly suffer some hairy moments. But if history holds, your patience should pay off as long as you wait long enough. On the other hand, a venture capital fund has a limited life span. Venture investors can't wait forever to profit. They have a horizon by which they either have to take a company public, find another company willing to buy it, or simply hang their heads and walk away. That pits them against a clock in addition to all the other barriers that can befoul a forming company.

In fact, the decade-long life span of a venture fund—in some cases it's even twelve years—is an acknowledgement that successful venture investments can take a while to ripen. "This is a company building process, and you need time to build companies," says Henry McCance.

Even the best entrepreneurs, backed by the best venture capital, usually have to hustle around both interior and exterior obstacles that arise to set back a start-up's gestation, birth, growth. Even the best business plans can't foresee them. They have to be resolved on the fly.

When Polycom incorporated in December 1990—behind backing from Jim Swartz of Accel and Bandel Carano of Oak Investment Partners—it had pinned its high hopes on a set of design assumptions that turned out all wrong. That was its internal obstacle. Sure, the company felt secure in its breakthrough concept: to make and market full-duplex speaker phones for businesses. Competing conference phones of the day were all half-duplex designs, meaning that the microphone and the speaker can't work at the same time. A half-duplex phone can send voices, or receive voices, but it can't do both at once. That makes for clipped and stilted conversations. Based on the company's original business plan, Polycom phones would let people enjoy more natural conversations, talking and listening at the same time.

So far, so good. But then the company started to stumble. Turning out prototypes, it learned that its first designs weren't likely to excite many buyers. One model was created to plug into the handset of a standard personal phone. But when a person then switched his phone over from personal mode to speaker-phone mode, the device encountered some rather serious "state-transition problems," in the terms of Brian Hinman, Polycom's founder and then its chief executive officer. If you hung up the handset after switching to group-talk, you cut off the call. "It was non-intuitive that you had to set the handset down next to the thing," says Hinman, an inveterate entrepreneur who is now chief executive of the technology company 2Wire, a 1998 start-up that develops gateways for delivering telecommunication services to homes. 2Wire's venture backers include Doll Capital Management, Oak Investment Partners, and Venrock Associates, in addition to Accel Partners, which previously backed Hinman at Polycom and, before that, PictureTel.

"At about the same time, some of our suppositions about what constituted a good table-top phone weren't working out either," Hinman says. Polycom had copied the general form of the AT&T half-duplex speaker phone it hoped to displace. The contraption split into three pieces: a separate keypad for setting up a call, a microphone tethered awkwardly to a cord, and a stand-alone speaker to place off on the side, presumably on a credenza.

"It doesn't make good, intuitive sense that the speaker and mic are separated," says Hinman with the benefit of hindsight. Listeners would automatically turn their heads to the speaker, making it tough for the mic to pick up their voices. To its embarrassment, Polycom learned of these shortcomings when it asked a big target customer to review the design. The chip-maker Intel was the era's largest user of audio-conferencing equipment, says Hinman. Therefore the fledgling Polycom listened carefully to its complaints.

"I remember the board meeting when we went through the problems," says Hinman. Polycom's management was stuck on trying to patch up the mistakes while retaining the design and development investments it had made thus far. "And Jim [Swartz] said, 'What the hell are we thinking here?' He said, 'Forget about the sunk costs. Let's shut the thing down and do it right.'" Recalls Hinman, "they [Swartz and Carano] said sometimes you have to zig and sometimes you have to zag. It was encouraging to hear the VCs say it's okay to be wrong. It's okay for you to make mistakes and be honest about it."

Polycom went back to the drawing board. The setback cost about six months of development time, says Hinman. But the resulting product swept the market.

But later, with sales humming and Polycom residing comfortably in the lead of the speaker-phone pack, an outside challenge appeared. At about the same time that Polycom made its Wall Street debut in 1996, a computer-modem maker called U.S. Robotics brought out a copycat product. It can be tough to sell shares to the ticker-tape watchers when your territory is being beset by a much lower priced, competitive version that's moving through highly visible, retail storefronts. "It cast a dark cloud over our financing," says Hinman.

Of course, at IPO time the last thing venture backers would want to see are dark clouds obscuring finances. Polycom launched a design-patent infringement suit, since the U.S. Robotics model looked so much like Polycom's tricorne talking box. According to Hinman, the suit froze up distribution of the rival product, because a Polycom victory could mean that anyone selling the look-alike product could also be found for patent infringement. It also helped that, according to Hinman, the U.S. Robotics phone sounded scratchy and distorted. Still, it took the company about two years to parry the challenger. Says the VC Swartz, "we put them out of business, which is not easy to do."

Determination pays not only after a venturer is inside a deal. It also leads places. By John Fisher's account, it was Draper Fisher Jurvetson's persistent commitment to on-line services—transactions conveyed over networks and delivered to consumers' computers—that led it, like the Yellow Brick Road, to early opportunities in Internet funding. And that was despite discouraging losses from investments in on-line services originating in the late 1980s. When Greylock was a mere youngster, in 1966 and 67, the firm made some forays in cable television, which was then just emerging. They didn't pay. But Bill Elfers and his two partners purchased some valuable lessons from the experience. One lesson was the difficulty of recruiting superior managers for small, insignificant operations, especially operations in limited markets that would never generate much revenue. Another was to be more wary of competitors. One of its three early cable investments, Beacon Cable of Newburgh and Beacon, New York, had waged pitched battle with another cable operator for half of the city of Newburgh.

Chastised but undaunted, the venturers held on to their conviction that cable TV was fertile territory. In 1970, Greylock found Continental Cablevision. Elfers writes that, as of 1995, "on a dollar-for-dollar basis, this has been Greylock's most profitable investment." Henry McCance sat on the Continental board for more than two decades.

Determination doesn't only expose a view of whole new industries. It can also bring a VC to individual opportunities that would wander away if not pursued with unwavering commitment, plus some hopeful optimism. Jacqueline Morby of TA Associates—who would be anyone's nominee for any award that rewards persistence—dogged BMC Software for a handful of years before its founder, John Moores, finally relented. "But just when I thought we were about to make an investment, I went to a meeting and discovered that they had sued IBM," recalls the veteran VC. "You can't go make an investment in a company that's suing IBM." That was in 1982. Undiscouraged, Morby carried on the courtship until the suit was settled in 1985. "If you find a really good company," Morby advises, "you don't let it go."

TA's investment totaled $7 million, with the aim of making BMC a public software company. Its IPO was completed in August 1988. John Moores, the founder and sole owner before the TA investment, fired himself as chief executive at the time of the public offering. He resigned as chairman of the board of directors in 1991. But not before the entire undertaking opened his eyes. A former IBM programmer and salesman, he had started BMC simply to sell the utility software he wrote to make IBM's popular, IMS database run better. "The last thing I ever thought about in the world was taking a company public," says Moores. "I had no more idea than a goose what I was getting myself into. But I never could walk away from what I thought was a good business opportunity." Apparently not. In addition to purchasing the Padres ball club, Moores helped start the venture firm JMI Equity Fund, operating from Baltimore and San Diego. Moores is a limited partner.

More recently, tenacious Morby wouldn't let go of SoftMed Medical Systems, an investment that TA finally made at the tail end of 1999. She followed the tiny concern for six years, stopping by to chat and catch up every time she came around its Bethesda, Maryland, home. This protracted introduction amounted to about fifteen visits, she estimates. Such calls are typically informal, says Morby: Hi. How ya doin'? What's new? SoftMed is the brainchild of CEO Donald Segal, who developed hospital software for managing patient records. Like Moores's creation of BMC, Segal's story is an old-style, from-the-bootstraps, office-in-the-basement account of entrepreneurial success. He began this business in 1983, and grew the company through sweat equity. When Morby first started calling, she says, "I wasn't sure if it would ever work out into anything, because he was only a programmer. Now he's grown, and he doesn't seem like a programmer to me anymore."

By 1999, SoftMed had grown large enough, and influential enough among hospitals, to take over distribution operations. That would mean a merger with its longtime distributor, Innovative Health Systems, a Sacramento-based company. "In order to do that, we needed capital," says Segal. The $47 million infusion from TA occurred the same day as the merger, in December 1999.

"Because I knew them for quite a while, and because of their persistence, I just got to like them, and I think they liked me," Segal says. But he is very clear that his choice of TA Associates for equity funding was based on more than just affability. "Over time a variety of VCs were knocking on the door, some of them a little more persistent than others," he explains. "Just knowing someone and liking them doesn't necessarily lead me to a business transaction. You need to know their business philosophies, and how they deal with other companies. Once the deal is done and the money changes hands, what happens?"

Thus Segal conducted extensive due diligence of his own on the firms courting his business, a process he stretched out for nine months. The exercise included meetings with principles as well as associates of the firms, and talking to the CEOs of some of their portfolio companies. "I wanted to make sure we had the right people," he emphasizes. That meant a partner who would stand by SoftMed even during rough phases. "I could see that other venture capital companies would have been very happy when you're doing great," he retells. "But when things are not quite as planned, they can be overly worried about situations without investing enough time to understand them."

Thus it was TA's history and its operating methods that eventually sold the firm to Segal and SoftMed. But he acknowledges that Jacqui Morby's six years of perseverance provided the foundation. "I thought from the beginning that these guys would be able to help us," Segal says. "In retrospect, given the other characters in the picture, we agreed this was the best choice to make."

Of course, most TA deals cook up a lot faster than its BMC and SoftMed buy-ins, says Morby. And some small companies that the firm courts persistently don't come through at all. "There are nice companies around that we've kept in touch with for years and nothing ever works, because they never do anything," she observes. "They just stay private forever, or decide to go public" on their own. Morby made about half a dozen visits to the high-flying software supplier i2 Technologies, which eventually went public without ever taking any institutional private-equity money. Back when today's celebrated VC Ann Winblad ran her own entrepreneurial software company, Morby had called on her. A deal never materialized between the two women. As often as that happens, persistence will prevent a committed VC from walking away from potentials that look to be only simmering—a lesson Jacqui Morby learned through a fair amount of persistence herself, since she started in venture capital, at TA, in 1978.

TA's investment focus on more established private outfits that have two feet at least partially on the ground—avoiding the fresh-cut start-ups that early-stage VCs go after—automatically aligns the firm with the traditional venture practices that were commonplace before the fast-acting Internet scrambled established habits. Through the 1990s at least, Internet companies didn't need to wait around and prove themselves in order to get investor attention. Almost from an Internet company's inception, valuation soared so high that late-stage investors found it prohibitively expensive to buy in. That leaves TA and its ilk to operate largely in the old economy: companies engaged in pre-Internet businesses. But among the faster moving, early-stage venture capitalists looking for ground-zero actions, persistence was sacrificed to the competitive hubbub. The feeling was that you needed to hit the target fast, the first time, or someone else would beat you.

Says Rick Burnes of Charles River Ventures, "in the seventies and eighties and some of the early nineties, you could set up a really good management team in a B market, and sort of like a heat-seeking missile they could hone in on the right market. Today, unless you go right to the heart of the market and execute, someone else is going to do it."

The collapsing time horizon forces VCs to alter some time-honored practices. Take the leadership search. No one will quite say that they don't want CEO's and corporate officers to be persistent, dogged, and determined anymore. But, says Burnes, "I think those kind of characters were actually more important twenty years ago than they are now." Today? "It's more important to be right." The flexibility to make on-the-fly adjustments, he says, is simply much more constrained.

But being right and being patient don't necessarily exclude each other. If the cutthroat competition to establish new companies has taken all the leisure out of the pursuit, that doesn't mean that even the right companies will strike gold as rapidly as they did during the boom market, when private-equity investors couldn't unload them fast enough to get back and fund the next.

Besides, if the race for the fastest running venture capitalists is to reach the highest flying entrepreneurs, the runners are likely to find that long-term thinking is an asset they can sell to some of the strategic thinkers they're so eager to back. Robert Young may not have been a typical entrepreneur when he was looking to line up venture backers behind Red Hat Software, the company he co-founded with Mark Ewing. In 1995, he was forty-four years old, and he was already an experienced hand at small-business management—though Red Hat was shaping up to be his biggest hit by far. Young says he selected Benchmark and Greylock because the two firms don't accept the accepted industry success rate: two big winners, four so-sos, and four write-offs for every ten venture investments. As Greylock's Kaiser puts it, if he has three children, he wants them all to go to Harvard.

"To get that win ratio, the guys at Benchmark and Greylock hold on to investments a lot longer," observes Young. "They say, we'll figure this one out eventually, and they know that sometimes it takes a little while. If you ask how many years does it take to build a good technology company, and you look at Hewlett Packard or Intel, it's a 20-year process."

9

CHAMELEON-LIKE QUALITIES

Adaptation is persistence without the time element—almost. In fact, the two qualities are inextricably linked. Determination and persistence mean staying in it through twists and changes. Adaptability is the willingness and wherewithal to turn the changes to advantage. Persistence alone can be nothing more than a mule-like ineptitude—determination to stay in the ring through every punch, through all the jabs, hooks, crosses, and uppercuts an opponent cares to bestow. It might be wiser just to take a fall. Adaptability incorporates the same, stay-on-your-feet stubbornness, but it also applies quick-witted response. You figure out how to counter the slugger, and start landing blows of your own.

Therefore persistence doesn't do a venture capitalist a lot of good unless it's accompanied by adaptation. But adaptation doesn't have to occur persistently, over long-haul episodes. It can also appear very early in an undertaking. When Scott Tobin of Battery Ventures started doing due diligence on Akamai, the plan before him was to create a software company, with Akamai packaging software that would enable on-line businesses to boost the performance of their over-the-Web services. But during a meeting between Tobin and the founders in a Battery conference room, a different idea landed on the table: model Akamai as a service provider itself, building the communications infrastructure that would enable it to perform Web enhancements on behalf of clients, charging them a recurring fee for the task. It would take a lot more capital to build a physical network than it would to simply sell computer code. But million-dollar software packages are a hard sell, anyway. And with Akamai providing the service, system setup and operation would be much easier for its customers—an incentive for them to sign on—while Akamai would be assured recurring revenues. Thus a fundamental change in the business model was hatched before Akamai was even a fully functioning company.

At the other extreme comes the case of Raxco, a software outfit that Jacqueline Morby of TA Associates financed with an $8 million equity investment in early 1989—a large infusion in those days. Five years later it underwent a change so radical, it required a name change, becoming Axent in 1994. Its recovery was certified complete in April 1996 by an initial public offering.

Accel Partners was also a part of the turnaround, purchasing equity beside TA in December 1989. Other venture partnerships bought in along the way. Arthur Patterson, Accel cofounder, joined Morby on the board of directors of Raxco, which sold system-management software tools. Basically, that's software that lets large-scale computing operations build controls for their systems for handling, say, the organization of data files, or coordinating on-line help services, or assuring security by keeping unauthorized users from tapping into a corporation's data-processing devices. Aided by some venture-led acquisitions to fill out its product line, Raxco grew rapidly, expanding from about $8 million in sales in 1989 to nearly $40 million just a few years later.

But Raxco software served VAX computers from Digital Equipment Corp. In their day, they were the dominant minicomputers, which are middle-sized machines scaled between large, powerful mainframes and nimble little personal computers. VAX boxes were favored by banks, manufacturers, and other businesses that had to handle a lot of transactions on-line. As popular as they once had been, by the middle 90s VAX computers—and Digital Equipment along with them—were succumbing to the relentless PC.

"We found ourselves in a company that had a huge customer base, and a great maintenance stream, but we could see that it was going to deteriorate very, very fast," says John Becker, Axent chief executive officer. Therefore the corporate managers approached the board with two proposals. The first was the most obvious solution: sell the company before it was too late. At least the investors would get their money back. "But we also said, there's an outside shot at retooling this company, and here's an idea: we have these little tools in the security space, and security is going to become more and more prominent," retells Becker, who was chief financial officer at the time, and an architect of the quick-change. "We laid out a very broad, far-reaching concept" to remake the company as a specialist in computer security systems, selling off unrelated products and focusing laser-like on software-controlling functions like password authorization, and firewalls that keep unwanted interlopers out of private networks. For all its uncertainties, at least the plan wouldn't require more financing. Raxco had about $10 million on its balance sheet.

Becker recalls: "Jacqui [Morby] said, 'I'm not in this business to break even. You're not asking us to put more money at risk. I think you guys should go after this opportunity.'"

The executives dashed out and refined the strategy, giving themselves one year not only to complete the transition but also to put the company on a strong enough footing to support an IPO. They feared personnel would begin to wander away to other companies if the change took much longer. What's more, says Becker, both Accel and TA were getting close to closing funds, which made them more eager for the returns. "We hit every milestone of that business plan," Becker exclaims. "We announced Axent at the end of 1994 and we went public in April of 96."

What attracted the support of the VCs on the board was the fact that the scheme was an entrepreneurial fix. "The market fell apart around us," says Becker, "and we said, this means throwing away everything we have today and starting from scratch. We thought it was very risky, because it was a brand new market. But we knew we had a lot of good people, and that's what drove it. VCs look for an idea, they look for a market opportunity, but I think most of all they invest in people," reasons the CEO. In the case of Raxco-cum-Axent, they invested in people who could adapt.

Whether applied all at once, like at Akamai, or developed while a company probes and experiments over a long duration, as Axent was forced to do, adaptation represents a young company's adjustments to the things that inevitably come up. It's the axiom of birth: Start-ups don't get everything right the first time. They have much to learn. While they're learning, circumstances change unpredictably in the undeveloped markets and new-tech sectors in which they operate. Therefore a venture capitalist, along with the entrepreneurs running any young company, must change the organization's business plan, its approach, products, personnel, and any other attributes that march out of synch with eventual success. Adaptability is a creative faculty that asks the question "What should we do differently?" It contains an element of humility since it requires a practitioner to admit errors. It mixes in persistence, too, in its willingness to confront errors with enough determination to fix them. As Jim Swartz points out about Polycom, it took physical prototypes, bought with a lot of costly engineering effort, to show that the company's starting assumptions about the form and the function of its speaker phones were fatally flawed.

"The team originally just mis-estimated," he says. "After we got into it a while, and we began to see it and touch it and think about what was going to happen, it became pretty clear: the initial product wasn't the right product. We found that we had to redirect and reposition it very significantly, on the fly."

It's as though you have to scramble up the near peaks first, before you even get a glimpse of the crags that wait beyond. Then you have to change course to accommodate them.

Of course, miscalculations can mar any investment. And certainly the surrounding environment can change—if nothing else, it can change as a consequence of the business cycle. Investment advisers tell clients not to chase the stock market, and not to try to time its rises and falls, but instead to sit tight through scares with the expectation that the market's resiliency will sooner or later bring back better times. But at the same time they'll call it prudent to reallocate some assets to correspond with the prevailing economic conditions. When stock markets turn bearish and more people are interested in selling than in buying equities, some financial pros say individual investors should move a bigger chunk of their assets to more stable safe-havens. That's an adaptation.

But in successful venture deals, the investor embraces strategy changes not so much as a fallback position but as a fundamental activity that's necessary to see the investment to a successful conclusion—and sometimes to turn a blandly successful conclusion to an astonishingly successful one. With new companies in new markets, too much is unknown at the outset. "When you buy stock in General Electric, you buy it with a different set of information than when you buy stock in two guys, ten slides and a dream," says Nancy Schoendorf. The presence of those unknowns changes a VC's expectations: She knows she'll have to get involved to make sure her investment makes inevitable, necessary changes. And if she's realistic, she admits that some of the changes may get rough.

In fact, as closely as it relates to persistence, adaptation as a venture-investment principle also holds hands with involvement. The whole reason VCs get involved in their investments is because they need to apply creative responses and flexible adaptations to the changes, surprises, and miscalculations that appear. In large measure, adaptations are the remedies VCs apply throughout their active involvement. Or to turn it around, involvement is the delivery mechanism for adaptations.

But there's no reason to stop with involvement and persistence when associating adaptation with other investment practices. It's also a dominant trait in the personalities that venture funders hunt for in entrepreneurs. After all, the VC may participate in the changes, but in most cases the business executives actually carry them out.

At Polycom again, Swartz credits corporate management and especially CEO Brian Hinman for the company's quick product change—and for some creative rearrangements that came later. After it straightened out its designs, the speaker-phone maker couldn't get hidebound communications-equipment distributors to carry its products. Therefore it set out in search of alternate sales channels. It started in catalogs, went to direct sales via telephone, and finally found a good outlet in the office-supply chains that were just then starting to spread. At the time Polycom adopted them, each channel was a new way to move business phones. "It was a challenging company that required a lot of board direction and entrepreneurial hands-on effort," recounts Swartz. "Arguably, I think in the hands of someone less capable than Brian Hinman, it would not have amounted to much."

In Seth Neiman's view, "this is an organic process: we're talking about creation. You've got to have somebody in the middle of it who is reacting to events. Every one of these companies faces certain death on a regular basis, and it's the personality of the leadership, and particularly the CEO, that either kind of jujitsues it into opportunity, or avoids it, or gets crushed and finds a way to recover and turn it into a great success. And the reason is because they're extemporizing."

In fact, a flexible and forward-looking CEO often does it on his own, initiating needed changes in advance of specific advice and input from the investor. After all, the chief executive is immersed in his company alone, whereas the VC is involved in six, eight, maybe even a dozen different portfolio companies. As many as a handful of those may be in a developmental stage in which they require a lot of hands-on tinkering and active involvement. His time is divided.

Mohr Davidow's Nancy Schoendorf gives Agile credit for finding its own way out of the networking technology transition that saw software moving from what's called a two-tier client-server configuration to a three-tier architecture. The three-tier design is the foundation of the Internet. But back in the middle 90s, when Agile started product development and when Schoendorf was its solo investor by virtue of her first-round buy-in, the two-tier setup was still the dominant way to construct software. Accordingly, network servers were the computers that stored the data. Clients—the personal computers wired to the servers—carried the business-logic programming that performed work on the data drawn from the servers. One of the configuration's biggest shortcomings is that all of the PCs on the network need to have the same client software if they're going to do the same kind of work. Agile was trying to help product engineers pass details about their designs to product manufacturers. To do that, both camps would have had to run the same client software.

Revamping its system to run on a three-tier network was the critical adaptation for Agile, which founder and CEO Bryan Stolle calls the foundation to the company's eventual success. It occurred because the company just happened to sign up some early customers who were beginning to use outsourced contract manufacturing on a large scale. The practice of hiring specialty manufacturers to make your products for you wasn't as commonplace then as it has now become in the electronics industry. But since Agile was lucky enough—and Stolle himself calls it luck—to stumble upon some of the method's early adopters, it saw right away that it couldn't expect different organizations to configure their PCs to work reliably as a two-tier network. On the other hand, a three-tier setup could work because then the separate personal computers operate more like simple terminals. The business logic that used to run on these clients is housed on a separate server—that's the additional tier. All the clients need is the means to dial into the server. On the Internet, which is just a great big computer network, that means is called a Web browser.

"It wasn't that we were smart," says Stolle. "The problem was right there in our faces: guys, your stuff ain't workin'. It took us all of about three weeks of doing deployments with these customers to figure out that two-tier client/server ain't gonna happen."

That was about the same time that Schoendorf began wondering independently if maybe Agile should adopt a three-tier configuration. When she mentioned it, she learned that her partner was already sniffing in that direction. "Once you have a three-tier architecture," she says, "the Web is a very small step." In fact, she was ready to recommend that Agile next develop a Web client, to enable its software's users to communicate over the Internet instead of over a private network. "But Bryan showed up at a board meeting one day and said, 'I've got the technical team cranking out a Web client. I'm going to show it to you.'"

You can make the case that Agile should have gone with the newer, three-tier architecture from the start, and saved itself the hiccup. After all, other software developers were using it at the time. Shouldn't a brand-new technology start-up have adopted cutting-edge networking ideas? But the advantages of a three-tier approach weren't as obvious in 1995 as they appear now, now that the whole world is wired to the Web. "With every architectural shift, people get caught in the middle," Schoendorf observes. Even though they didn't get it right when they popped out of the box, Agile's leaders proved their worth when they recovered. The organization responded quickly to its software's shortcomings because it was plugged into its customer's needs, and it was attuned to changes occurring in computing technology at large. Similarly, Schoendorf picked up the new approach through on-the-job exposure. "Companies started to come through here and describe their three-tier architecture and I very quickly came to the conclusion that this makes a lot more sense than a two-tier architecture."

Ann Winblad says it best: "When you see a lot of entrepreneurs, you audition the future every day."

It's easiest when a venture backer and entrepreneur spot a looming detour together—or spot it separately but at least at the same time, as Schoendorf and Stolle did. After all, the CEO and management team must make the operational adjustments. In his advisory role, a VC who wants a company to change course is left to suggest, convince, and cajole. A lot of VCs adopt a Socratic method: ask the right questions, to help lead the entrepreneur to the desired conclusion.

In 1999, Celarix saw the deregulation of ocean-freight carriers as an opportunity to bring them into an on-line marketplace where they could arrange contracts with shippers like the cataloger L.L. Bean; retailers Abercrombie & Fitch and William Sonoma; Sharp Electronics; and other such shippers that use Celarix services to organize and manage their material-movement operations. To make the marketplace successful, Celarix would need active participation from both carriers and shippers, which are the sellers and buyers of the shipping logistics business. A Web marketplace, or exchange, is an Internet service that buyers and sellers visit to set up contracts. It wouldn't pay for buyers—shippers like L.L. Bean—to show up if sellers of the service—ocean carriers like Evergreen, Maersk, and Sea/Land—weren't there to offer their services. But Celarix received only a tepid reception from the carriers.

It turned out that the sailors were using old-fashioned, manual business processes; they weren't automated enough to take advantage of the Web market's efficiencies. In fact, participation in the Web exchange would likely end up costing them money when they added the administrative burden of translating between it and their antiquated business systems. But at the same time it would drive down their prices. At least that's the usual consequence of an open-service exchange. It would make their prices for hauling more transparent to their customers, and that would give bargaining leverage to the companies paying to have their goods shipped. "It's tough for them to make the transition, and you had to have for them lots of additional value on the exchange," says Izhar Armony.

That additional value turned out to be new software that would make it easy for the shipping companies to computerize their business practices when they joined the exchange. The software belonged to the company Management Dynamics Inc. (MDI), itself a start-up that was just a couple of years old. Celarix acquired it, and bundled its software into its own to attract the ocean-goers.

Armony figured into the adjustment in three ways. First, he played Socrates.

As a VC investor, board member, and interested yet detached party, he says, "you have the advantage, not of being smarter, but of seeing different companies, and having some common experience from Charles River, and not having to actually execute. So you have the benefit of being in a way an observer. But that is your advantage." In the case of Celarix, he goes on: "I said, hey, this is what's going on: we are behind business plan. Why? We're not getting good traction with the carriers. Why? They are afraid. What can we do? We have to add more value. What do we do?"

The reply, acquire MDI, came from Celarix itself, following a suggestion from one of the carriers that Celarix was struggling to recruit.

Armony says it was also important for him to allow the corporate executives breathing room to find the solution. He could have made the team sweat. After all, Celarix was performing below its own business plan's projections, he notes. But Armony considers that somewhat of a hallmark of a good start-up, as though lagging performance is an inevitable consequence of the abounding enthusiasm that accompanies any undertaking that's bound for success. "All entrepreneurs are extra optimistic," he explains. "If they are not optimistic, they are not entrepreneurs. They are working for IBM or whatever." He may not expect every portfolio company to fall behind its business-plan projections, "but you accept, and you participate in what it takes to be successful. You are not behind them with a whip. It's more like, you know, how am I to be helpful today? Give me a task. What am I to do?"

In the case of the MDI acquisition, Armony was to do a little wining and dining to cement the deal—an appropriate assignment for the foreign-born venture capitalist. Short, trim, energetic, more skin than hair on his pate, Izhar Armony engages people with his directness and his sincerity. But he also displays a comfortable playfulness. He enjoys himself. He enjoys his job. It satisfies him. Armony's English, as a second language, remains a bit disjointed. But he carries the deficiency with charm and aplomb. "I am an Israeli," he says. "I can claim that my English is not that good." He herded

MDI's founders into the large conference room at Charles River's offices outside of Boston. In that room hangs the honor roll: the framed prospecti of the firm's so-called billion-dollar club, made up of former portfolio companies with a market capitalization that has reached at least $1 billion. "I said, 'you guys now own hundred percent of a little company called MDI. True, I'm only offering you a percent of Celarix, but Celarix, we think, will have the right to be hanging on that wall.' And the guys looked around at it and they saw great names like Vignette and Excite and Sybase. And they said, hmmm, makes sense."

Armony then helped Celarix CEO Schumacher with some of the mechanics of the acquisition, since it was the young business founder's first.

Adaptations don't occur only to fix problems. Changes can also augment unanticipated victories. When John Fisher of Draper Fisher Jurvetson made the firm's first investment in Selectica Inc., in July 1997, the start-up was planning to peddle its software at the lower- to middle-price range for what's called "configuration systems." Manufacturers of complex products with a lot of mix-and-match features and options use configurators when they're taking orders, to make sure the particular combination of parts a customer wants can all fit together. It could prevent a car buyer from ordering an overhead console as an option on a model with a convertible top, for example, although as a rule the conflicts that configuration software solves are less obvious, like making sure a computer is equipped with enough cooling and a power supply adequate for the processors packed into it. Selectica's Internet Selling System was actually a new take on product configurators. It was entirely Web based, and it was intended not just to put together valid combinations of product parts, but also to guide Web-shopping customers through the entire purchasing process. The company initially priced the system at a range of $100,000 to $200,000. By comparison, the market's leading supplier, Trilogy, sold systems that ranged into the millions of dollars. And they required a lot of special tailoring to set up and install for each company that bought the software.

With the come-on of the Internet, Selectica's ideas for making it easier to sell complex products on-line couldn't have been better timed. It also helped that, as Web-built software, the system demanded a lot less setup and management attention from its users than did earlier-generation, competing configurators. According to Fisher, the Internet Selling System rapidly acquired a greater following than both founders and investors had expected. "It was much easier to maintain, much cheaper to use, highly functional, better than anything else out there," the VC enthuses. "As a result, we started to price accordingly. We added functionality that the other guys, who had been in the marketplace a lot longer, already had," to justify the up-market pricing. In the eighteen months between January 1999 and the middle of 2000, says Fisher, Selectica had not lost a sale to a competing configurator system. The company attracted more than $31 million in venture funding, completing later rounds of financing that included Draper Fisher Jurvetson as well as other firms. At its initial public offering on March 10, 2000, shares listed at an offering price of thirty dollars. In middle July, four months later, Selectica stock traded on Nasdaq at around seventy-five dollars per share. The company's market capitalization exceeded $2.5 billion.

Fisher gives credit for the business-boosting strategy change to Selectica's management, including founders Raj Jaswa, chairman and CEO, and Sanjay Mittal, the chief technology officer who began tinkering with what's called constraint-based configuration processing—the foundation of Selectica's Internet Selling System— when he was a scientist at the Xerox Palo Alto Research Center in the middle 1980s. "We were a sounding board for them as they had to think through the decision," says Fisher. But he'll point out other instances in which new strategy concepts come from the VCs. One is the creation of the "viral marketing" attachments that helped speed the adoption of Hotmail, another Draper Fisher Jurvetson investment. Credit for that idea is attributed to cofounder Tim Draper. When the free e-mail service was starting up in 1996, he persuaded the company to automatically stamp its advertisement to the bottom of every e-mail sent out by Hotmail subscribers. The aim was to encourage the message recipients to subscribe to the service themselves. To make sign-up simple, the ad included a click-through URL that would take each recipient straight to the Hotmail Web site. "Every customer becomes an involuntary salesperson simply by using the product," writes Steve Jurvetson, the firm's third founder, in a white paper. "Viral marketing is more powerful than third-party advertising because it conveys an implied endorsement from a friend."

Six months after its launch, Hotmail hosted about 1 million subscribers, according to Fisher. About two months later, the figure doubled. By the end of 1997, eighteen months after its debut, the e-mail service had signed up more than 10 million patrons. Eventually Microsoft acquired Hotmail. Reports put the purchase price at about $400 million.

In both those cases, the adjustments didn't correct deficiencies. Rather, they improved the portfolio company's position. Unlike stop-gap adaptations that are meant to fix problems—frequent necessities—changes meant to make a successful company even more successful can bring the stellar investment returns that place venture capitalists in the top tier. The aim isn't so much survival and simple success. After those, consistently successful VCs steer toward get-big, get-rich opportunities that appear in the course of a company's development.

Seth Neiman of Crosspoint wasn't content to let Brocade simply hum along as a stable and established supplier of computer equipment. The use of networked computers was growing exponentially, another consequence of the bounding Internet. The need for rapid and reliable transactions between servers and storage systems could only increase demand for products like Brocade's storage-access switches. It would be a very good market to own. But to drive the company there, Neiman needed to effect a drastic management change, replacing the CEO who had taken the reins from Neiman himself, after the venture capitalist had launched the company as a Crosspoint incubation in 1995. Even back then, Neiman had developed a strong conviction that Brocade could become a kingpin, maximizing its revenue by vanquishing competitors in its market. But by 1998, he felt that the company needed a leader with a different set of skills who would push it harder. It had successfully negotiated birth and adolescence, both worthy accomplishments. To get it to the next stage and thereby fulfill his vision for Brocade, Neiman wanted a chief executive who would "put his knee to the throat of competitors and force his way to the dominant position." The search led to Greg Reyes. Replacing the top dog is always a traumatic experience for a company, and therefore fraught with risk. But Brocade has prospered after its leadership change.

Fully successful companies don't stop at just plain good. That was the message Sequoia's Mike Moritz delivered to Bryan Stolle when he spurred Stolle to demand more from Agile's product collaboration software.

"About eighteen months or so into the company, it was becoming apparent that Agile was going to be a nice company selling a decent product," Moritz explains. "But there's a big difference between a nice company selling a decent product and a company that has a chance to become a really, strategically entrenched part of its particular business segment.

"I remember saying at a board meeting, the question now for Agile was not whether it can become a good company, but whether it can become a great company. That was the challenge. It was an accomplishment to become a good company, because lots of companies get started and they don't even have the opportunity to become a good company. Not many companies have the chance of becoming a great company." Meeting the challenge would require Agile to redouble its product efforts, rather than gloat complacently over its early successes. Observes Moritz, "the difference between a good company and a great company begins with the product and the services that you provide to the customers. You don't become a great company if you don't have a product or service that really does a tremendous amount for your customers."

Of course, Agile itself had to execute the upward adaptations needed to make its system indispensable to the companies that use it. "Our business is a business in large part of persuasion and suggestion," Moritz says. "You have to persuade the people who are responsible for running a company that your arguments or opinions or views have merit." In the case of Agile, "Bryan listens very carefully. I'm sure there were things that I suggested along the way that he thought about and discarded because he didn't think they made any sense, or they were impractical. But this one, for whatever reason, resonated with him."

That's a return to leadership qualities, the facets of personality that in Stolle's case were so tough to recognize at the beginning, only because he hadn't yet had an opportunity to demonstrate them. Surveying back, Nancy Schoendorf sees that the quality in Stolle that first convinced her to plunge into the deal was his fundamental business ethic. "Bryan has a set of values that I believed at the time matched well with the kind of values I have about the companies I want to help," she explains. "Bryan and I agreed early on that we were going to build a company where we had a 100-percent referencable customer base. That our customers were all going to be happy. That we would not have to be picky and choosy about who we said owned the product. We were going to do it right. We were going to take the time, make the investment from the very beginning."

Stolle took the goading to improve Agile's position because it was already in his nature to improve Agile's position. "I don't think the concept of a 100-percent referencable customer base was something I introduced to him," she continues. "While I may have articulated it, Bryan was thinking it. He had that value. He also had a set of values about how he was going to hire and manage people. So what you could see in Bryan, if not necessarily when we made the initial investment but over time, was somebody who had a very clear set of values that could build a company, and who was thinking two or three steps ahead. People like that are able to figure out a path that allows them to continue to build products and services to satisfy customer needs, and grow into a larger and larger company."

In a good CEO, flexibility and adaptation are qualities that come built in.

As an operating principle in venture capital, adaptation doesn't apply only to venture-backed companies. The venture firms themselves that have any history behind them manage to prosper—or maybe sometimes just survive—through up times and down by recognizing that as businesses themselves, they also have to conform to changing business dynamics.

That's been going on for some time. Charles River's subtle rejiggering of its criteria for selecting the most promising entrepreneurs—favoring strategic accuracy a bit more over dogged persistence—is an adjustment to the fact that dead-on strategy people are simply more likely to succeed today. It's the same with the long-running dash toward more focused, higher levels of specialization. "At Charles River over time we have gotten narrower and narrower," says Rick Burnes, the firm's founder. "In the eighties we had a much broader approach to where we could make money, and to where our strengths were."

In June 1999, TA Associates realigned its long-standing, profitable policy of putting its investment dollars into more established companies, which are less likely to belly flop since the concerns' founders and managers have already built sturdy foundations beneath them. The approach was locking TA out of a lot of meteoric Internet investments, because hot companies in that sector weren't sticking around long enough to ripen. Venture firms doing early-stage investing were getting all the action.

"We had a planning session and decided that we would make, maybe, ten Internet investments in earlier stage companies," recollects Jacqui Morby. "Well, before you knew it, we'd made six. I mean, they're so easy to make. There's nothing to look at. You have to commit in a week and close in a month. You used to make an early-stage investment and you'd be in it for eight years. Now you make an early-stage investment and you're out of it in six months.

It certainly is throwing everything out that we've ever used as a measure for what's a good company," she says. "But we have to."

The change isn't a radical realignment. TA shifted only about a quarter of its investments into early-stage Web plays. "We're not jumping full feet into the Internet world," Morby notes. "We think there's still a place for well-managed, profitable companies growing at thirty percent, forty percent a year."

And if the public market's antipathy for Web-incorporated IPOs changes the rules again, TA can always shift back to its traditional practice, which would constitute another adaption.

10

SHOWMANSHIP

Count marketing among the adaptations that venture leaders have made in response to their industry's own competitive intensity.

"If you had asked me five years ago if it was remotely possible that Charles River would be marketing to get into projects, I would have said, absolutely not," asserts Rick Burnes, who cofounded the firm in 1970. But now that venture capital has attained a high profile, a lot of other people are clamoring to fund the same power-entreps that Charles River wants to back. To win their attention, the practice needs to promote a positive image. "There's so much capital around that we're forced to adapt, to adopt a differentiating strategy," says Burnes.

Showmanship in venture capital entails all the activities other industries employ to get attention: public relations, media pandering, promotion, brand building, marketing, advertising, and sometimes just audacious behavior.

They're pursued for two separate purposes. One is to call attention to portfolio companies, to help them get a leg up in their own industries. The other is to build the image of the venture firm itself, to help it get a leg up on competing venture capitalists. That can help portfolio holdings, too, since some of the glitz of a high-profile venture capital firm rubs off on the companies it finances. This glamour by association has some practical benefits. For example, the PR agencies and recruiters of highest repute will go to work more ardently for little unknowns that bear the imprimatur of a venture capital leader.

As a rule the technology markets are hotly competitive themselves, and a typical start-up company has only a small and obscure voice. A lot of introductory technologies are obscure to begin with. Many are completely unheard of, since they're the bold, new, optimistic creations of the tiny companies hawking them. It can help to have a big-name venture backer holding a pointer to them.

"Increasingly promotion and buzz are what define an industry leader," notes Battery Ventures general partner Oliver Curme. For that reason, Battery now lists promotion as one of the primary value-adds it provides to its portfolio companies. In 1999, it hired promotions pro Dick McGlinchy to advise portfolio interests. McGlinchy boasts of twenty years' experience in PR and marketing, concentrated in the high-tech industries. At Battery, he's called a "special partner."

Mark Dempster, informally called Sequoia Capital's "brand capitalist," joined the firm in April 2000 to advise holdings on how to acquire name recognition, or how to build up themselves as a desirable brand in the eyes of their customers—or eventual customers. This is a new service from Sequoia. Dempster stops short of doing actual PR, marketing, and related chores for the portfolio members. For that he refers them to professional PR agencies, ad agencies, and the like, drawn from Sequoia's lineup of preferred service providers: agencies it sends repeat business to.

"A lot of my work is helping the portfolio companies define themselves," says Dempster. "Define who they are, what they do, what they stand for in the minds of their customers." He shuttles among the seventy to eighty companies in Sequoia's portfolio, which span across multiple funds. Naturally, the companies are in different stages of development, with different identity-development needs. "The bulk of the work centers on the newest portfolio companies with the shallowest of resources," says the image consultant. "They have some wonderful talent in the founders, but they don't have background in this area." Dempster came to Sequoia from his own small brand-building agency, Brand Knew, which he started after twelve years in corporate identity and brand-strategy practices.

Dempster is also charged with polishing the image of his employer, Sequoia Capital. That responsibility approaches the second role that promotion plays in the venture business: boosting the image and standing of the firms themselves.

Showmanship wasn't always a part of the venturer's calling—at least not overt showmanship purposefully pursued. When the private-equity business was smaller, and the deal-making pace was slower, its adherents operated more in self-contained, clubby circles that relied largely on word-of-mouth to make a firm and its activities known. VCs were silent hunters, and a lot of deals arrived simply through their own private and professional connections. In his book on the formation and ascendancy of Greylock, Bill Elfers cites investment after investment that the firm hunted up on its own. For example, in 1980 it learned of the biotech company Genetics Institute through Walter Cabot. As head of Harvard Management Corporation, Cabot looked after the disposition of Harvard College's endowment, which is a Greylock limited partner. Seven years and about $1 million after it bought into Genetics Institute, Greylock distributed its common stock to limiteds at a value of $12 million.

A lot of deals still arrive by recommendation. That's how Nancy Schoendorf first caught wind of Agile. Izhar Armony found Celarix from a tip by a business analyst at AMR Research, a consulting firm he respects. Jacqui Morby heard of SoftMed from a hospital administrator who had run the information services department of Georgetown Medical Center, where SoftMed's software was used. As in any other business, for an entrepreneur hunting up a venture partner, it's who you know that helps open doors. For a venture capitalist, notoriety helps assure that promising entrepreneurs want to open theirs.

Of course, conspicuous success is always the best PR. Anyone who knows anything about venture capital can tick off the name Kleiner Perkins Caufield and Byers, no matter how convoluted the verbal construction, and despite the fact that venture capital appears nowhere in the title. John Fisher of Draper Fisher Jurvetson— a firm with a name only slightly more accommodating to the tongue—notes that Kleiner Perkins climbed to its preeminence through about twenty-five years of persistently successful deal making. That still must be the preferred method of notoriety building for companies that started with Kleiner Perkins back in 1972. But few did. Draper Fisher Jurvetson, for one, started life in 1985 as a solo operation headed by Tim Draper. But it really didn't get rolling until Draper's partners joined him about five years later.

"To some extent we have been able to short-circuit that 25-year cycle through marketing and advertising," Fisher claims. The aim has been to build Draper Fisher Jurvetson's name into a recognized and respected franchise, largely by staying in the headlines. It's a tough assertion to absolutely prove, but Fisher suspects that his partner, Tim Draper, was the first VC to actually advertise—a move that elicited scorn from other venture players for its rank commercialism, says Fisher. That was back at the very start of the 1990s, in *Upside* magazine, which Draper takes credit for starting. Today the firm does a column in *The Red Herring,* the magazine that chronicles the start-up scene. It also appears willing to go to attention-grabbing extremes that others might consider undignified. To illustrate a June 1998 *Red Herring* feature titled "Free Mail Explosion"—about Microsoft's acquisition of the Draper Fisher company Hotmail, a purchase that parlayed into a very big gain for the practice—founding partners Tim Draper and Steve Jurvetson posed beside a burning postal box, wearing expansive grins and charred, shredded business suits meant to look like they had been through a Loony Tunes explosion.

"The old adage that *perception is reality* is true," Fisher argues. "If the perception out there is that you are an active firm, and the press writes about you so you are in the news, then you must be a

player. You must therefore be connected. You must be an interesting place for an entrepreneur to go to to get financed. If you can get
yourself written about in the *New York Times,* you can probably
get me, the entrepreneur, written about. And that's true. We probably can. We can help, at least."

Fisher is quick to note that his firm is not trying to run on
ephemeral image alone. In the end, he contends, investment results
have to back up the company's claims. "There has to be some meat
on the bones." But by making the firm's results more apparent, the
windy advocacy can help assure that promising, high-powered entrepreneurs will call on it.

"It makes it much easier if you're a deal magnet, rather than if
you're getting on airplanes to go to every darn trade show and
every conference, and pulling out the telephone book to start making cold calls," John Fisher says.

Of course, one catch with that approach is that a high-visibility
firm doesn't get just the good deals coming in with its mail. It gets
all the deals. After all, every entrepreneur considers his concept a
sure-fire winner. They all think of themselves as the most capable
managers. Each expects his company to become the next Intel, Apple, or Amazon. Draper Fisher Jurvetson runs a triage system to
handle the volume. Associates brush over the 15,000 to 20,000
business plans the firm receives each year. Only about 1,000 of
them get a second look. From those, somewhere between 500 and
600 eager entrepreneurs are invited to the harbor-side office to
make presentations, says Fisher. That's when one of the partners
first starts to give a team a serious look. On any business day,
Draper Fisher Jurvetson is hosting from three to five or six prospec-
tives. Some of those are return visits, for the few that pass muster.
The ranks winnow rapidly, since the firm ends up investing in only
about fifteen new companies per year.

"We're busy," Fisher breathes. "Nobody said it was easy."

Burnes calls the horde of unsolicited business proposals he receives "fodder for the delete button," since most arrive via e-mail.
Many are broadly cast proposals, anyway—mass mailings sent to

every VC with a published address—and they're all published. Venture-practice Web sites are artfully designed both to convey a positive image and to make it easy for entrepreneurs to contact the firms. Burnes jokes that a lot of the over-the-transom business plans that Charles River receives are addressed, "Dear Mr. River."

The firm prefers to fund repeat-entrepreneurs with proven abilities, and those people are already known, says Burnes. In a lot of cases, they may be talented, compulsive business starters who have done deals with Charles River in the past, established a reputation and rapport, and then returned for another go. Therefore the firm's marketing aims not so much to attract deals but to maintain its reputation so it can close the deals it wants. That is, so entrepreneurs will feel like their doing business with a firm that has substance.

Of course, not every new business it backs begins as an established relationship. But instead of taking walk-ins, Charles River prefers the recommendation-and-reference approach to finding first-time entrepreneurs. Izhar Armony wasn't just idly chatting with the AMR business analyst when he heard about Celarix. Armony was actively out shopping for a Web start-up that focused on shipping logistics. He had already identified the market need, the opportunity, on his own, as he acquired his VC's knowledge of the B2B marketplace. He had been talking to industry insiders about the field. One day he got a phone call from his business acquaintance from AMR, suggesting Armony talk to Schumacher, Celarix's cofounder.

Thus, in some ways, some successful venture capitalists remain silent, solitary hunters. In fact, some avoid the limelight altogether. McCance says that before consenting to the interview for this book, he routinely refused to speak to media inquisitors about Greylock or the venture capital trade. (And the fact that he consented this time shows another adaptation: Even venerable, tight-lipped Greylock has decided to court at least a little public exposure.) Instead, he banks on reputation.

"My belief is that the people who count, the engineer sitting at Microsoft who's got an idea and wants to go start his company, the engineer or marketing VP at Yahoo who wants to do it, they are pretty well plugged in to the whole venture capital process and to the entrepreneurial process," says McCance, who thinks very hard and very seriously about this stuff. "And therefore, they do not need to see a lot of newspaper stories to know who the real tier-one venture capitalists are. They know it. It isn't too hard to know that John Doerr at Kleiner Perkins is a world-class venture capitalist," McCance illustrates. "We don't need a lot of publicity. My partner Roger Evans was the CEO of a successful data communications company called Micom Systems. He then joined Greylock [in 1989]. He was the sole venture capital director of Xircom, a successful datacom company in Southern California. He was the founding investor of Ascend Communications, which was built up to $20 billion in value and sold to Lucent. He's the lead investor of Phone.com, which is one of the hot new wireless companies that's public. If you're a data-com engineer, you know that Roger Evans is somebody you would love to have on your board. Is there a list of two or three others in the venture industry with that resume? Yeah. Is there a list of 25? I don't think so.

"Having a lot of press about Greylock, and about Roger Evans isn't going to increase the deal-flow of the people I want to come here. What it might do is increase a lot of deal flow from people that I don't want."

Still, Greylock's reticence lands it in the minority among venture firms. No one keeps count of how many outfits engage in some kind of marketing or promotion, but the practice has grown commonplace. For most firms, the question today isn't so much to tout or not to tout. Rather, it's to what degree should the firm sell itself.

"I think every firm has to do some level of marketing," begins Nancy Schoendorf, the Mohr Davidow partner. But she feels that some go so far overboard that their portfolio companies may bear the cost. "Some marketing techniques take an enormous amount of time and energy. But you only have a finite amount of time and energy." The logic: efforts spent strutting and shouting will leave less resources for value-building involvement with portfolio holdings.

In fact, at its farthest extreme, image building has even begun to influence the makeup of portfolios. "Showmanship often requires that you do high-profile deals not because they are good investments, but because they get your name in the paper, and in theory they bring you other deals," Schoendorf says. "There are some firms that in the last couple of years have really set themselves apart with showmanship," she charges. "I don't know if that works or not. I'm pretty skeptical. It means that there are investments on which you're going to take a lower return because you've done it for the name impact."

She suggests a middle ground between glamour venture capital and Greylock's steadfast reliance on reputation: By focusing on sound investments and on coaxing them to consistently successful outcomes, a VC will accumulate results that speak for themselves— with perhaps a little look-at-me image building to help out. "I think you've got to market yourself as a firm, but then really put the majority of your effort and resources into focusing on good deals, and not compromising your standards simply for a deal that's got great name recognition," she says.

"They are two different philosophies of firm building," notes Schoendorf. "It's a little too soon to tell which one is going to have the better returns in the long run. And in the short run, showmanship hasn't been proven to give great returns." Schoendorf expects better investment discipline to return, with chastened VCs no longer chasing deals for headline value alone. But it may not happen until the industry cycles through a couple of funds that yield unacceptable returns. "A lot of people in the venture industry have never seen anything but great times," she points out.

But for as long as they last, the pursuit of stardom will continue to rankle the venture business. Fisher complains that professional jealousy motivates some competitors to deride his firm. "Part of it is because we rose out of relative obscurity and into the limelight in three years, from ninety-four to ninety-seven. I think a lot of it has to do with the very high-profile, outspoken, sort-of maverick character of my partner, Tim Draper. Part of it has to do with the precocious and attention-grabbing nature of my other partner, Steve Jurvetson." Fisher himself is a serious-minded thinker who looks to be the least audacious member of the trio.

"In both of their cases, it's about business," he defends. "It's good for the firm to have a high profile. It's part of our strategy. But that's going to invite some animosity."

Fisher and company deserve some credit for at least wearing their aspirations publicly. Others appear a lot more guarded about boosterism—and that's probably the best evidence that the venture community for the most part remains uneasy about blatant promotion.

For instance, when Ann Winblad jumps so quickly and insistently to defend her firm against any suspicion of self-interest, it's a good guess that Hummer Winblad gets regularly chided for horn blowing, and that the accusation stings her professionally. "We don't have a PR firm," she states. "We are one of the few venture capital firms that does not have a PR firm, even though we are highly visible. Our visibility comes from our accomplishments, not from making PR firms call up journalists."

Undoubtedly. But image-making is an accomplishment that doesn't always depend upon the gloss and hustle of a PR firm. If professional achievement alone induces high visibility, then you would expect to see a greater number of firms ranking above Hummer Winblad in the limelight queue. Hummer's portfolio of sixty-four software companies—the number listed as of spring 2000 in the firm's promotional brochure—doesn't include any of the stand-out, legendary investments that have grown into household names. Eventually some may. For the most part these are still young companies. More than half of them are Internet software houses. Hummer Winblad was founded only in 1989, when Ann Winblad joined the profession and teamed with John Hummer, who has been a VC since 1982. But as of today the portfolio includes no accomplishments that approach Henry McCance's Continental Cablevision, or Don Valentine's Apple Computer, or even the more recent Yahoo buy-in by Mike Moritz, Valentine's colleague at Sequoia.

Yet Ann Winblad turns up everywhere. To the popular media she's become a kind of cover girl of the technology business. By media standards she is a logical choice. Winblad is photogenic, bright, eminently quotable, stylish, willing, and cooperative. If Hollywood decided to do a venture capitalist who is spunky and vivacious, it would have Meg Ryan do Ann Winblad. She even tells her own Cinderella story about starting a software company, called Open Systems, with a paltry $500 investment, then selling it six years later for $15 million. In those days, venture capital didn't back software start-ups, she says, and in the beginning she had to put her programmers on food stamps. Today her name bylines a regular column in *Forbes ASAP,* another breathless, digital-business periodical, which Forbes passes out to subscribers of its regular business magazine. She was listed as one of the 100 most influential people of the digital era by *Upside* magazine. *Vanity Fair* placed her among its top fifty leaders of what it called the New Establishment. *Business Week* picked her as one of Silicon Valley's twenty-five elite power brokers. Not to be left behind, *Time Digital* put her on its list of high-tech's fifty so-called Cyber Elite. Most recently, the May 2000 *Forbes ASAP* profiled her among sixteen luminaries it called "the world's best VCs." The picks also included McCance, Moritz, and Valentine. But that last honor hardly seems to count for Winblad, since she is a regular contributor to *Forbes ASAP.* Ann Winblad is outspoken, energetic, determined, and irrepressible. You have to assume that she would make any bookish editor within her circle very uncomfortable about excluding her from a list of the world's best.

"She's a great personal publicist," offers Jim Swartz, the founder of Accel. But as for her reputation as the primo female VC, he suggests some others whose professional achievements ought to give them great visibility as well—if investment prowess was the sole criterion for media stardom. His list includes Nancy Schoendorf. And he calls Jacqui Morby "one of the great investors over a long, long period of time." Of course, it's doubtful that *Vanity Fair* is interested in Jim Swartz's nominations.

His remarks are dispassionate, uncritical, and offered only as an explanation for why some of his colleagues among long-established VCs may resent Ann Winblad. It's easy to imagine a competitor envying her ability to attract a spotlight, even without the help of professional image men.

Her prowess shows up plain as day in the firm's March Madness contest, which wrapped up in March 2000. Actually, the program's name changed to February Madness when the National Collegiate Athletic Association got after Hummer for appropriating the title of its intercollegiate basketball playoffs. The promotion took place on campuses, after all. But Ann Winblad still prefers the original title, recognizing intuitively that March Madness simply has a better ring to it than does February Madness. The contest aimed to tap the entrepreneurial talent emerging from 100 universities across the United States. It asked for business plans. Partners then scurried to the various regions of the country to assess the entries. The final four teams flew to San Francisco as guests of Hummer Winblad on March 21, the first full day of spring 2000. The winners—students from the University of California at Irvine, with a plan for a company called Drugrep.com—got funded to the tune of $5 million.

Was any of that promotional? "We don't write checks for promotional reasons," Winblad replies.

True enough, the rationale behind the contest makes good sense. "We needed to expand our reach into the best incubators in the world, which are the universities," she states. The VC counterpoises that to the popular practice of recycling entrepreneurs, by backing experienced start-up artists in the expectation that they'll do it again. "This guy's a money maker; let's back him," she mimics. "Yes, there is truth to that. But there is also truth to the fact that markets are changing. To really make sure that you are funding the pick of the litter, versus just looking at the same thing, we really have to work hard to expand our reach. We really think that everyone is prone to suck on their own exhaust fumes and, guess what? That kills brain cells."

But February Madness was still a contest, and like all contests it conveyed elements of blaring brass bands and good-time carnival games, along with some of the you-bet-yer-life suspense of who's gonna win the big prize. It's the sort of event that newspapers from small-town local rags to big-city dailies like to hang stories on. And with contestants vying from 100 scattered campuses, a lot of rags and metro dailies are in play. There are quieter ways to mine for latent entrepreneurial talent hidden in dorm rooms. Like lecturing, the way John Doerr of Kleiner Perkins addresses members of Stanford University's Technology Ventures Program. Like sponsoring mentoring programs, such as the Mayfield Fellows Program at Stanford, underwritten by Mayfield Fund, a thirty-year-old venture practice on Sand Hill Road. Or, if it must be a contest, firms sign on to support established competitions, like sponsorship of the Harvard Business School Business Plan Contest from Battery Ventures, Chase H&Q, Highland Capital Partners, J. H. Whitney & Co., Polaris Venture Partners, and RRE Ventures.

Besides, are universities really the best places to begin a search among the cherubs for the next Billy Gates? The few legendary, prediploma whiz kids who became lasting technology moguls walked off campus on their own. That's much different from getting nudged out front of the student union and asked, "hey kid, you want five million bucks?" VC after VC attests that spotting budding corporate leaders is their toughest task, even when they're evaluating entrepreneurs who have logged some real-world business experience. How accurately can even the most prescient VC assess kids whose greatest stress in life so far has come from the approach of midterms and finals? Who knows. It's possible that the student-creators of Drugrep.com will one day turn up on a *Forbes ASAP* list of the world's best entrepreneurs. Still, take away the $5 million and you have to wonder if, in effect, these kids weren't set up for an eventual fall.

But whatever becomes of the investment, the February Madness fete stands as the most effective kind of promotion. Ann Winblad's innocent denials notwithstanding, it grabs attention like a carnival barker—but it does it a lot more subtly, because it manages to be legitimate work at the same time.

As image building and promotion, that's a first-rate accomplishment. And such execution is bound to elicit envy from any competitors who can't match that level of performance. But sooner or later, markets demand results. In time, any venture capitalist who's raising a new fund to make future investments will have to show how the returns from past funds beat what the VC down the street pays. Newspaper clippings won't hurt that. But alone they won't be enough to persuade limited partners to pony up cash for another round.

11

THE BALANCING ACT

One of the most sensible and enduring tenets for consumer investors and even the pros reduces to the simple old saw that kids pick up in kindergarten: Don't put all your eggs in one basket. Few children today spend time in a henhouse. But still the meaning is clear: diversity. As an investor, be sure to own a little of this and a little of that, so if this tanks, you'll still have that. And if this or that really soars, you'll hold part of the action.

In fact, it's diversification that pulls so many consumers into mutual funds. Buy-for-sport day traders aside, it can be too risky for ordinary Janes and Joes to purchase stock in a sole company. If that company sputters, their precious nest egg goes the way of H. Dumpty. But given the limited, sometimes paltry sums they can put into the market, it makes no sense for them to try to spread it around, buying a couple of shares here and a few there. That's a lot of bother. Brokerage fees start to add up. And the returns from owning, say, two shares of Krispy Kreme doughnuts will never amount to much, anyway, no matter how much the stock moves. A mutual fund merely leaves the spreading around to a professional, who can buy a lot of shares of Krispy Kreme because he's using the pooled resources of a lot of customers. Each consumer gets the se-

175

curity of a diversified portfolio in a vehicle that's as easy to manage as a passbook savings account.

Of course, the whole market may crash, and sometimes it does. Diversification won't insulate an investor from an across-the-board belly up in equity values. That's when persistence may pay more, because in time the values return—at least they always have in the past.

A venture capitalist is closer to the mutual fund manager than he is to the pick-your-own stock shopper, especially if you're talking about the manager of a focused fund. Restricted in investment territory, he sets out to make the best picks within his specialized interest. Sometimes the focus can be very broad, like large-cap equities or small-cap equities for a mutual-fund manager, or Internet companies, computer software suppliers, or communication equipment makers for a venture investor. But aside from some mixing and spreading out of equity stakes within a specialty, a VC concentrates his investments only in the fields he expects to pay the headiest returns.

In modern venture capital, balancing an investment portfolio entails some limited diversification. But you don't hear much about spreading bets just for the sake of maintaining a fallback position, with some investments stuck out in an unknown territory just because, well, they might pay off. Instead, firms attempt to protect their portfolios first by doing enough homework and staying well enough attached to new developments that they can confidently predict the business fields that will bring home high returns.

Next, among the leading players at least, they make individual investments only in companies they're convinced will grow large, very large, yielding generous rewards for their early backers. It's never enough to shrug, *This one should do okay*. Before a top-tier firm invests, it feels very confident that the company it's backing can travel to the sun.

Third, balancing a portfolio gets down to a safety-in-numbers game. The aim is to take positions in enough companies—and especially in enough of those plum deals that you expect to soar—because, of course, not all of them will. Miscalculations occur. A firm needs at least a few headline successes for each fund to hoist its value and compensate for any laggards. To get them, VCs make sure they don't place too many eggs in too few baskets.

More than scattershot, trans-industry diversification, the hedge for venture investments is the activity VCs undertake to assure success for their holdings. This is active investing, after all, with the venturer applying specialized skills and resources developed around the needs of the assets, young companies, which require leadership selection, involvement, persistence, adaptation, and the rest. But even so, not every one will grow into the enduring giant its investors anticipate.

"Even though most of our companies grow, and become profitable, and prosper, there is still a very skewed distribution of returns, where the top few companies in any one of our funds generates half the returns," points out Oliver Curme of Battery Ventures. You hear the same story elsewhere.

"In a typical large venture fund, you're going to invest in maybe 40 companies per fund. Our experience is that two or three of those will probably return 60 percent to 70 percent of the total of the fund's returns," echoes Tom Dyal, the Redpoint cofounder. "They won't return the whole thing. And it's usually not one, but usually two or three that generate 50 to 60 to 70 percent for the whole fund. And of the other 37 companies, another 10 or so of those will make up the bulk of the remainder. And the rest, well, they end up being profitable. I mean, 90 percent of our companies end up making money for us." But they don't push the dial far enough onto the plus side to elicit wild cheers from the audience, which is the limited partners who put up the funds.

If venture capitalists were fortune-tellers, maybe they wouldn't bother with the tepid returners at all. They could go straight to the two or three superstars, mix in the handful of strong supporters, and dump all their money into those alone. But, of course, they don't know until after the game who those stars will turn out to be.

As Curme puts it, "we're out on the edge trying to build companies that are going to play a pivotal role in reshaping industries.

And sometimes you really get it right and you get something that's worth ten billion or more—maybe a hundred billion. Sometimes you just build a good company that's worth half a billion."

Since those *really right* investments are the minority, if a firm isn't trying to find one every time it puts down its money, it's less likely to get the two or three it needs. "If you invest in 40 companies but in your mind only five of them really have a shot at being big, and the others just look like good investments, it makes it hard to hit that home run," reasons Dyal. But swing for the fence each time, as the analogy goes, and "there's a better chance that you'll have one or two or three of those home runs." Accordingly, before Redpoint buys a piece of a company, the partners sit down around the white board to make "the ultimate guess," in Tom Dyal's terms, "at what the market cap of the company could be." As experienced venture capitalists, "a lot of times we can't quantify whether it's a billion or ten, but we know it's a good idea."

So it's not just herd instinct that has driven just about every insightful venture capitalist since about 1997 to make nearly all their investments in companies that relate one way or another to the Internet and the Web. Those companies are paying the most today, and highly successful venturers need to be where the payoffs are greatest. It makes little sense to make a play in, say, biotechnology if newly formed businesses in that sector aren't paying off very handsomely, and most VCs agree that the sector hasn't returned well for quite a few years—although the stock-market performance of some public biotech companies began to see some encouraging upticks early in 2000, and although some VCs still list it as their specialty. Still, unless a venture investor is convinced he has future vision that enables him to see what everyone else is missing, it's hard to justify a token investment in biotech just in case. Sure, the company might do okay. But the VC isn't looking for okay, and he doesn't have to accept okay as long as he has a high-growth sector like the I-net to absorb his fund's dollars.

To some extent that concentration of venture resources follows from the nature of scientific and technical development. It feeds itself, with breakthrough leading to breakthrough, with a new idea in one quarter stimulating a follow-up innovation from another, with fundamental knowledge and capabilities acquired at the start of a movement supporting later-arriving developments, which support the ones that come after those, which arrive all the quicker as the knowledge base grows, and as more and more people are lured by the expanding opportunities. The other noteworthy new industries of the postwar century started in the same fever of development. It happened in semiconductors and microprocessors. It happened in biotechnology. And now it is happening in data communications. With apologies to Al Gore, no one decided that the late twentieth century would be a good time to invent an Internet. It occurred because a lot of foundational circumstances allowed it to. It occurred because the communications infrastructure—basically, the telephone network—had matured enough to support it, and because computing technology had done the same, and simply because personal computers had become so widespread that they encouraged the exponential growth of a universal network. The collection of interconnected computers became more useful to its members each time another PC operator installed a browser, and its redoubling usefulness encouraged still more people to hang their PCs onto the network, increasing its power yet more.

Therefore, as much as the VC next door forces every other venture player to specialize—in order to beat the neighboring VC to the deal—the very nature of their calling, finance for new tech, forces venture capitalists to run in more or less the same direction. During the buildup era of a new technology, that's the direction that promises the highest returns. In the case of the Internet, which reaches so far, changes so much, and combines so many technologies itself, a lot of VCs expect the fever to burn for about another decade. They expect it to create a lot more opportunities before it's officially declared saturated and mature.

"When we find an area we like, we want to do more of it, and we try to add to our portfolio in that given sector," explains Jim Swartz of Accel. Rather than timidly picking and choosing invest-ments to achieve a portfolio that's balanced and spread to protect against losses, the firm dashes aggressively toward its conviction.

According to that approach, success hinges on the correctness of one's conviction. Surely experience helps a well-established practice like Accel get it right. Swartz himself has been a VC since the 1970s. But care and deliberation seem to be the strongest factors supporting the firm's confidence. Accel does enough brain work up front, before leaping into a segment, to finally leap without fear that it may overexpose itself in its enthusiasm. By its reckoning, it's entering an investment for the right reasons, not just because it's following the crowd. Swartz points out that Accel never made an investment in pen computing. Despite the cheers and excitement that greeted the idea of PCs that people could write on, the veteran VC and his partners figured the concept would fizzle as rapidly as it did. But before it did, when just about everybody else in Silicon Valley was funding a pen start-up, says Swartz, "we sat around and debated it for hours, and finally just said no, we're not going to do any." That's also how Accel stayed out of any advertising-sup-ported consumer dotcom companies, even though it considers itself an Internet-investment specialist. It went after the segments of In-ternet technology and Web service that it considered legitimately valuable, in spite of the frenzy around it.

With concentrated investments, overlap becomes a concern. "We don't like to get so narrow that we have two companies that are really in the same business, or are dealing with the same cus-tomers," says Battery Ventures's Curme. "It puts us in a conflict of interest position, it's just awkward, and it's not a good business practice."

But that doesn't mean it won't fund close relatives. Battery's star investment Akamai provides Web content distribution for its cus-tomers by using a land-line network it built. Later, Battery backed the company Edgix. It also does for-hire content redistribution, but it uses satellites to make the connections. Similarly, Battery has equity stakes in two business-to-business systems integration companies, which are contractors that build e-business systems for corporations. But one operates on the east coast and the other on the west, "and the market is so big that they never see each other," says Curme. The arrangement allows Battery to reuse its experience and expertise in that business sector in support of both investments.

"If we see a theme that we really want to ride," Curme explains, "we'll pick a company in the middle of it that's maybe providing services. And then we might pick some product companies and some companies in adjacent markets. We try to find ways of playing that theme as much as we can without generating a conflict."

Similarly, Draper Fisher Jurvetson made a lucrative run behind a series of e-mail companies. But in one case, two of its portfolio holdings became head-to-head competitors when one learned how well the other fared. The way the story's been reported, Draper had to erect what it calls the Chinese Wall between Four11 (spoken "four-one-one") and Hotmail in 1996 and 97, after Four11's management decided to expand the company into free e-mail à la Hotmail. Four11 started life as a Web directory that enables people to search for long-lost college classmates, and others less remote. Hotmail was the pioneer free e-mail service. When the entrepreneurs behind the two start-ups met through their mutual sponsor, the Draper firm, they set up a partnership that made Four11 the Web directory used by Hotmail subscribers. That link gave Four11 a look at the explosive growth Hotmail enjoyed by giving away e-mail boxes. It decided to play the same game.

To avoid the obvious conflict, Draper Fisher Jurvetson initially tried to dissuade Four11 chief executive Mike Santullo from expanding into e-mail. But the market was simply too tempting for the CEO. The venture firm adjusted by assigning separate partners to the boards of the two companies—Tim Draper to Four11, Steve Jurvetson to Hotmail. They then took care around the office to avoid compromising conversations about either company. Four11 ended up selling to Yahoo, in a transaction valued at about $90 million at the time. (It's the current people-finder function inside the Yahoo Web site.) Afterward, Microsoft paid about four times more for Hotmail, according to reports. Nevertheless, John Fisher says the Four11 sale turned out to be more lucrative for the firm, because of later appreciation in Yahoo's stock price.

In other cases, the firm's string of e-mail–related investments didn't require as much cloak and dagger. Companies like Digital Impact, a marketing service using e-mail; NetZero, an Internet service provider that includes free e-mail; and Tumbleweed Communications, an e-mail delivery service for documents, operated under different corners of the e-mail blanket. "We went and broke it up into six or seven or eight ways to take advantage of e-mail," says Fisher. "It was one of the hot-buttons in our investment strategy, and so far we've made money on it every time."

That's the goal after all: to make money, and to make it in copious sums. Nowhere is it written that a venture capitalist's aim is to avoid losing money. And while that may be implied as part of the undertaking, the fund structure that the industry follows seems to take care of it automatically.

"You don't win or lose on each investment," explains Rick Burnes, the Charles River czar. "You win and lose on the whole portfolio. You can only lose one times your money on any one investment, so that your downside is capped. But your upside is not capped at all, so the see-saw is very heavily tipped toward the winning side." Statistically, a portfolio should almost automatically contain enough companies paying positive returns—at multiples high enough above the original buy-in—to cover any write-offs for other companies that don't survive.

"Even in the worst of venture-capital times," continues Burnes, "prior to the '90s, no venture capital firm ever lost money. Even firms that do a terrible job just don't lose money—unless somebody steals the money or something. If you have more than about 13 investments, blind pigs make money."

Thus investment security in venture capital reduces to a game of numbers. Back enough companies and, according to the mathematical nostrums of probability and statistics, you'll nail enough winners to keep you in the black. The question then becomes, how many is enough?

Firms have their own comfort threshold. Charles River averages about ten new investments per year. Typically a firm takes several years to fully invest a fund, at least for the portion of a fund reserved for first-time buy-ins. Resources also go into reinvestment in follow-up rounds for companies already in a firm's portfolio. Venture firms that are comfortable with mathematics settle somewhere between twelve and fifteen companies to fill a portfolio.

"You can answer the question with statistical techniques," explains Battery's Oliver Curme. "What you find is that if your portfolio has only two companies in it, it's kind of risky. A lot of times those two companies might not do well. And then once in a while one of the two companies will hit and it will be a fantastic portfolio. But it's not a good, balanced portfolio. But once you get above 12 companies, you don't get a huge amount of benefit from additional portfolio distribution. Once you've got 12 companies, the odds are that you're going to get at least one, maybe two huge hits that generate a lot. Then you'll have a bunch of good companies, and some companies won't do well. So there's no reason to have more than those, to go from 12 companies to 20 or 30 or 40."

The reign of probability theory opens the door to passive portfolio management. That means leaving investment returns largely to luck, without much of the value-adding hustle that leading venture practitioners apply to try to up the odds of success—as well as to increase the level of success. The passive approach assumes that if the firm's dollars are spread among a sufficient number of up-and-coming companies, even if the investor adds no value whatsoever, the odds are good that he'll still get the winners he needs to lift the overall portfolio and erase losses from any individual underperformers.

The practice works best in boom times when breathlessly gullible, later-coming investors pay large for pieces of practically any company a venture firm brings to the public market—the way

they did in 1998 and 1999. But veterans never expect those conditions to last. Besides, the goal of the most successful VCs isn't just
positive returns or even respectable returns. Their goal is eye-pop-
ping returns that pay back ten times the original investment—the
coveted *ten baggers*—and sometimes fifty times, 100 times or more
above their original stake. Investments that double and triple a
VC's original pay-out won't place a portfolio among the fabled big
winners. That's why the venture investing methods and principles
are applied so assiduously by the top-tier firms. For one thing, they
can boost returns, making the big wins bigger, and giving more
portfolio companies a shot at coming in a big winner. Burnes reports that, of the approximately 100 companies his firm backed
through the 1990s, only two actually lost money.

For another thing, industry-leading VCs want to back only the
young companies with the strongest shot at growing to be billion-
dollar enterprises. That means they have to sign up only the hard-
est-working, most promising entrepreneurs. But the proven and
most promising entrepreneurs aren't interested in teaming with investors who only sweat them for returns. Consistently successful
VCs score more often because they attract the entrepreneurs most
likely to score. To do that, they offer them more than just dollars.

12

DAREDEVIL RISK-TAKING

When Bob Young was scouting for financial backers for Red Hat Software, he put VCs through a little test. He sat them down and explained that Red Hat is a software company that gives away its product. After all, Red Hat more or less gets the stuff for free itself. It distributes the Linux operating system. Conventionally, software is created, sold, and controlled by a single company. But as open-source software, Linux is public property. Every line of code that comprises the operating system is published. There are no patents or hidden kernels of source code that enable a software vendor to protect the thing as its own. But that's considered the principal strength of Linux. On account of its open source, it gets developed, tweaked, and improved by an informal, unaffiliated, international army of digital enthusiasts who pull the system down from the Web and tinker with it in their own time, for love, not for money. The only rule is that any purported improvements to Linux have to also be published on the Web, free and available to all. That enables every member of the worldwide community of Linux lovers to judge the value of a change, and appropriate the ones they find worthy. That adds up to a lot of independent minds that are continually improving the software.

Consequently, Linux has a reputation for being bullet-proof. It just doesn't crash the way Windows operating systems are known to fail. It's also considered very elegant, clean, and efficient by the people who pay attention to operating systems. Those people include corporate information-technology executives, who are the guys in charge of the computers at General Electric, Ford, and on down the list. Very many of them prefer to run their all-important Web servers on Linux. Not only is it very reliable, but as open-source software, Linux also gives them control of the code. Commercial software users, who employ a lot of bright programmers of their own, can open up the operating system and change it around to suit their needs specifically. You can't do that with Windows or any of the other proprietary, closed systems.

Bob Young saw that attribute—user control of the programming code—as a big advantage that would catapult Linux to popularity among corporate computer pros. His plan for Red Hat was to establish it as the premier brand of Linux, the same way Tide tops all other laundry detergents, and Heinz is the first choice for ketchup. Red Hat programmers improve the Linux system (publishing their upgrades), and customers can either download it for free from the Web, or they can purchase a copy on a low-cost disc from Red Hat. Either way, the company promotes its Linux-related support and services business, and it builds its reputation as the best place to come for the software.

But the venture capitalists who approached Young—the calls started in 1995, when Linux started to stimulate industry buzz—couldn't get past the fact that Red Hat was giving away its product. How could it ever make money?

"I was looking for partners who genuinely thought they could face the challenge," says Young. "If they weren't willing to step up to the challenge, then they were the wrong VCs. I understood that the opportunity was based on delivering control to our customers. I didn't want to be backed by a VC who would cause us to corrupt that model. I was quite prepared to alienate a VC and send him away."

Most went away willingly, shaking their heads.

"They could not see that there was a business here because they were too programmed in how the software industry worked," says Young. "Our whole business model is based on changing how the software industry works."

That's a pretty big change. In fact, it's a change of such dimension that it is fraught with risk. But Benchmark and Greylock did not walk away from Bob Young's challenge. Kevin Harvey, the partner who brought Benchmark into the deal, says he viewed it as "having high risk with breakout potential." But he seems almost to minimize the peril presented by Red Hat's new selling approach when he points out one of his biggest concerns: "recruiting management in Raleigh, with a small local pool, was a risk."

It turned out that tapping executive talent became a minor issue, largely because of the existing rapport between Bill Kaiser, the Greylock VC who coinvested with Harvey, and Matthew Szulik, who Kaiser brought in to be the top manager. Red Hat proved to be attractive enough to lure other executives as well. "I'm proud of the fact that we were able to get the CFO from Adobe, Harold Covert, to move three-thousand miles and buy a house in North Carolina," he illustrates. "That speaks highly for the value and the magnitude of the opportunity." Adobe, located where San Jose anchors Silicon Valley, is a very well-established software company. Covert left it in 1999 to join Red Hat.

Kaiser also underplays the risk associated with the Red Hat investment. "It was high risk from the standpoint of an unproven business model," he begins. "The main risk was, what would open-source bring? And would it be a flash in the pan, or would it be a lasting trend? But it was lower risk than some situations, in that Red Hat had an established business that was up and running. There was some management structure in place. There were developers. They were shipping product. So there was very little risk that they were not going to have any revenue, which sometimes is the kind of risk that we take in companies."

But to Red Hat cofounder Young, Harvey's and Kaiser's cool regard for the uncertainties involved in the deal spotlight the daring that makes them premier venture capitalists. "The reason they are top-tier VCs is because they think forward. They think beyond what the current opportunities are," he says. "This was massively risky in the sense that I was not 100 percent sure how this business model was going to evolve. I could give them a whole series of revenue streams that we were focused on exploiting, but I did not know at the time which would be the revenue streams that would take us to $100 million or even $1 billion worth of revenue." But as Young watched them, both Kaiser and Harvey boldly looked beyond the uncertainties. "They valued the correct things at Red Hat," says Young. "You make money by having customers, and they looked at the world-wide customer base we have that is expanding rapidly. There's got to be a way to make money in this, which is why I wanted those guys in this corner."

Specifically, he wanted them in his corner for their collective expertise in discovering how to turn companies to profit. Benchmark and Greylock bought into the deal in late summer 1998. By late summer 2000, the saga of Red Hat was still playing, but every scene so far hinted at continued success. Upon Red Hat's initial public offering in 1999, its stock started out at $7 per share. In December that year, when the Nasdaq stock market was still euphoric, its equity became what Young calls "the flavor of the month," trading at about $150 per share. But as 2000 scorched through summer, it settled down into the $20 to $30 range, bouncing better than most tech stocks over the potholes that pitted the uncertain market at the time. Significantly, Red Hat was tracking toward $80 million in sales in 2000, and Young said the company remained on track to fulfill its commitment to Wall Street: an annual doubling of revenues for a few years running. Harvey and Kaiser see the ultimate fate of Red Hat tied up in the arrival of Web computing. The expectation is that the software loaded into personal computers will grow unimportant, because PCs and even network-dependent *Internet appliances* will eventually pull the programming they need from the Web, taking only what they need, only when they need it. In that scenario, the servers powering the Web become all important. Web-server operation is where Linux shines. "Linux is the operating system of the Internet," asserts Harvey. "In my view, that means focusing on the server, with the client [PC] increasingly marginalized."

It remains uncertain when, how, or even if Web computing will fully materialize. But an obscured future doesn't frighten off intuitive VCs when they sniff out the arrival of a big change. Discontinuities, the sundering of old ways by newer, better approaches, are the places where they earn their greatest returns. If they don't dare to seize them when they first appear, they'll languish back with all the other also-ran VCs who only follow trends.

Daring is an element of all investing. Okay, maybe the guaranteed government bail-out of banks removes the risk from ordinary savings accounts for consumers. But growing passbook balances is more an act of squirreling than it is honest-to-goodness investment. Investing involves putting money in places that you expect to become more valuable tomorrow than they are today. That may be a grassy field where someday someone will want to build a mall or a housing tract or maybe yet another golf course. It could be equity in a blue chip that other investors will want to own more desperately after it extends its brands into other fields or gambles into a big spurt in market share—perhaps by discovering that people are willing to drink even more old Coke from the vehemence with which they reject new Coke. It could be a commodity, like gold or wheat, that people will want more tomorrow than they do today. In all investments, the risk is that the thing—property, equity, commodity, Beanie Babies—will decrease rather than increase in value. Maybe circumstances change, like new government land-use restrictions that prevent you from plowing up your property. Maybe more information comes to light, like a midnight discovery that the land parcel sits on an ancient Indian burial ground. Maybe your first assumptions prove just plain daft. People might not have wanted any Coke, old or new. As a consequence, you lose money. In extreme cases you might lose all of your money.

In venture capital, the investor takes an inherently risky position in anticipation of a higher return as compensation. The high risk rate comes from the many preinvestment uncertainties presented by new ventures. Management is very often unseasoned. Markets may be unformed. Technology can be untested. Often it still has development to undergo before it even can be tested. Entrenched, well-financed competitors stand ready to squish any newcomers who step onto their turf. Of course, the high reward potential of a start-up is proportional to its high risk, since risk and reward are two sides of the same coin. The uncertainties surrounding a venture investment grow out of the fact that it is something brand new. But because it is brand new, when the company takes off, its value multiplies significantly, because it started at such a low-value point.

That equation drives top-tier venture firms toward higher levels rather than lower levels of risk. Most often, the mega-returns that put them on top come from the break-away ideas that are clouded most by uncertainty, simply because they're so unprecedented. "Those great opportunities aren't everywhere," observes Redpoint Venture's Thomas Dyal. "There's only a handful, maybe 20 or 30, that come around a year. You have to get your own fair share of those if you're going to be a top firm." With every other ambitious venture firm after the same plum deals, that doesn't leave much of a cushion for indecision.

Of course, the investment methods of venture capitalists aim to reduce their risk—or at least to give them a shot at managing it. Activities like leadership selection, active involvement, adaptation, sector knowledge, and all the others operate around the understanding that small-growth companies need a lot of help and they require a lot hard work as they scramble past the considerable perils they face. But none of those methods assure success. In the end, a venture investor needs boldness enough to operate even in the face of considerable uncertainty.

"You have to take a leap of faith. It is kind of a roll of the dice. That's why they call it *venture* capital," says Jake Reynolds of Technology Crossover Ventures. To him, the gamble involved in a venture investment remains particularly acute, since Reynolds is still somewhat of a greenhorn. But even old-hand practitioners who have made the leap many times acknowledge that the profession reduces to intuition above any analytical knowledge. Working on intuition requires the boldness to move in the absence of objective certainty.

"This is a skill that you cannot learn out of a text book, and that you can't learn by going to business school," says Henry McCance. "Really the only way to be a great venture capitalist is by doing. You learn by doing. That's why I like to think that good venture capital is one of the last trades in the investing economy."

When Seth Neiman conducted his preadmission analysis of the venture business, picking apart Crosspoint's portfolio to find the keys to successful venture investing, he discovered a second factor that correlates across all winning picks. In addition to a top-notch CEO, big-hit investments start out with what he calls red flags. "Great investments have risks of several different kinds, and they show up as red flags. You don't know this; you don't know that," he explains. "And when you step back and think about it, of course that's true. If there's a big prize to be won, it probably is hard to get. Sometimes you can make risk-free investments, but they will not be big winners, not even with a hyperbolic stock market."

In a way, the built-in risks simplify investment decision-making, inasmuch as they remove a lot of the analytical burden. Instead of straining the brain, the process wrenches the gut.

"First of all, there isn't much data at the beginning of a venture. And things happen very quickly," Neiman observes. So the decisions that you have to make are very simple: is this a giant market; is this a world-class team; can a start-up win. That doesn't mean those are easy decisions to make. But the actual questions are not that complicated. And you can't expect to analyze your way there. This will be an instinctive decision."

It adds up to an intimate partnership with risk that requires a successful VC to make ample room for it. "Given some of the crazy things that we do, I'm not sure that we have a risk threshold," says

Michael Moritz, the partner with Sequoia Capital who rolled the dice on Yahoo. He explains that the firm stops short of acting foolhardy, but when it perceives a promising opportunity, it doesn't fret excessively over the risk of failure.

Indeed, a sense of derring-do is so vital an element of successful venturing that some firms institutionalize procedures designed almost to insure they remain intrepid. Redpoint approaches a deal as a balance sheet of pros and cons, examining factors favoring an investment versus factors weighing against it. "Obviously in the ones we do, the pros strongly out-weigh the cons in our minds. But there are always cons."

At Draper Fisher Jurvetson, the rule is that if any two partners give a thumbs-up, the firm goes ahead with a deal. That means five of its seven partners may oppose it. "It's a structural risk threshold that we assume that maybe no other venture capital firm does," says John Fisher. On the other hand, he points out that the way it works in practice, Draper has never gone into an investment that a majority of its partners strongly opposed. The character of a partnership prevents anyone from going too far out on a limb. "You don't want to lose political points with your partners," notes Fisher. "If you are consistently losing money on deals, you won't be a partner for long." Still, investments are made over dissenting votes. "You may have two guys against it and three fence sitters and two for it," he says. "That deal gets done. Our proclivity is to take the risk. We do not fear losing money on any individual deal. The most you can lose on any given investment is one times your money. Losing one-times the money has no impact on the outcome of a portfolio. We sometimes invest in a company where we think the chance of losing our money is over 50 percent, because the reward potential is so huge that if the thing hits, we make a billion dollars for the fund. Then we do it. We take huge risks."

It's not like there's no way out of a deal—though it may be true that there is no graceful way out. Money once invested can't be taken back. But by refusing to do a follow-up round, an early investor sends a tacit signal that a company is a bust. Usually the company just withers after that.

"If the VC decides you need to go, basically your access capital just got shut off," explains Bryan Stolle, the Agile Software founder who is a close student of the Silicon Valley business dynamic. He's been through three start-up experiences, and the first two didn't work out nearly as well as Agile. Than means he's lived and learned through both successes and a few mistakes. "The VC is really in that position, unless you convince some other VC that the first VC is full of it, which is really hard to do."

That's one aspect of the VC-to-entrepreneur relationship that can really rankle business founders, especially ones who have seen their finance channels dammed. Still, it's tough to imagine that a company's founders and managers are in a better position to assess their business prospects. "Usually management is saying, 'hey, if this folds, I'm out of work,'" relates Jim Hynes, the former head VC of Fidelity Ventures. "So if you put more money in, they'll keep going, saying, 'maybe something will happen.' And sometimes it does," he concedes. But more often, it doesn't.

Failures are simply a part of new-business venturing. They can frustrate a VC even when prospects look most promising. In his book *Greylock: An Adventure Capital Story*, Bill Elfers tells how his firm missed the transition of computer hardware from a specialty market, in which newcomers could profitably exploit a market niche with special-purpose machines, to a commodity market, in which one-size-fits-all computers gave the edge to large, mass-production manufacturers over fleet-footed entrepreneurs. The oversight cost Greylock more than $6 million, which Elfers calls the company's largest portfolio loss ever. The culprit was a 1986 investment called Stellar Computer. By all early indications, Stellar was a good bet. It was created by a proven management team that was headed by entrepreneur Bill Poduska, who had been the technical brains behind Prime Computer and who had later started Apollo Computer, both profitable Greylock investments. Thus Greylock met its own first rule of successful venturing: back good business leaders. But this undertaking never quite got off the ground. Aside from some internal problems, especially technical holdups that prevented it from getting its high-performance computers onto the market quickly enough, Stellar became caught up in a price war with a rival hardware company it hadn't seen coming. Worse, the expensive, high-performance chips at the heart of Stellar's machines began to be undercut by readily available, general-purpose microprocessors that provided nearly as much computing power at a fraction of the price. Hardware had simply moved on.

In hindsight, writes Elfers, Greylock might have seen it coming. Advances in computer hardware were coming so fast that next-generation machines were taking over one-time market niches before venture investors with a position in a niche could capture their financial rewards. "There is no sure thing in a technical start-up, even one with a great pedigree," he writes.

VC's don't talk very much about their retreats. Pride is one big reason. They also have a healthy fear of lawyers, in cases where the owners of a failed business might want to start pointing fingers and filing lawsuits. It's hard enough just to know when to back out of a deal.

"A lot of times you may not be willing to do it yourself, but that's what your partners are for," says Edward Kane, founder of Harbourvest Partners. "You know it's time to get out when your partners tell you it's time to get out." After all, they can look at a situation from a detached vantage that enables them to consider the overall position of the firm. The partner leading the investment is likely to have close ties inside a questionable portfolio holding. What's more, his own tenacity and one-more-try optimism might further disqualify him.

"It's the nature of this business to make mistakes. To do things wrong. To screw up," says Kane. "If you're not able to accept that, you're probably in the wrong business."

After all, some failures come inevitably as a consequence of daring investments. Knowing that fact enables firms to make the occasional quixotic gamble on the supposition that it just might pay off big. Despite its strong conviction that consumer retailing across the Web is in large measure a loser, Charles River made two investments in business-to-consumer, or B2C, ventures. "One of my partners thought it was a good idea to test the waters, and I'm a great believer in testing the waters," says Rick Burnes, the Charles River founder. "We're going to lose five, six, seven million dollars in that market, and that's fine."

It would be a far greater sacrifice if a venture practice was to give up its decisiveness to act. J. Neil Weintraut, a founding partner of 21st Century Internet Venture Partners, characterizes risk taking as the simply propensity toward action, toward overcoming the inertia of immobility. He puts it like the Nike advertisement encouraging athleticism: "You just have to do it."

In his view, many people in the investment community back in 1995 recognized that the Internet was arriving like a comet bent on collision. No one knew exactly what they should do about it. Therefore most did nothing. But a handful of people frenetically raced to catch it. "There were probably millions of people who had the right vision. There were many people around the world who thought about it. On the other hand, there were probably only 100 or 200 who did something about it," says Weintraut. At the time, in his pre-VC days, he was a partner at the investment bank Hambrecht & Quist, which became Chase H&Q in a December 1999 merger with Chase Manhattan. He acquired a conviction about the Internet's power firsthand, by using Edgar, the electronic reporting system set up by the Securities and Exchange Commission. Operating over the Internet, Edgar collects and makes available the quarterly reports, annual reports, and other financial documents that corporations are required to file with the SEC. The reports are a staple of the investment banking business. But when they existed in paper format only, they had always been a burden to acquire, says Weintraut. With Edgar, he could get them instantly, without ever leaving his desk. "I saw that this was going to change every industry," he says. "Since February of 94, I haven't been the same."

As early as 1995, Weintraut chaired the first Internet conference for Wall Street. By his account, he shook up the established order inside Hambrecht, setting up and running its Internet practice, which helped establish the bank as a leading underwriter of issues in new-economy companies. But his ardor and insistence rankled a lot of colleagues along the way. "My attitude was, the worst they can do is fire me," he says. "I was passionate about it. I was going to do something about it, and I was going to do something about it with or without H&Q. But going through it is one hell of an experience, every step of the way. There are no guideposts, and it is not clear that it is ever going to go anywhere."

The difficulty with just doing the bold and decisive act is that it often flies in the face of logic, rationale, standard practices, or accepted knowledge. But prominent VCs report that many of their most successful decisions veer from the expected course. When Seth Neiman of Crosspoint decided to bring in a new CEO for Brocade, he was already crossing the grain. Brocade was on its feet, bringing in bucks. Standard practice called for another round of venture financing. But Neiman detoured, determining that a more aggressive person at the top was more important than the cash.

"The executive team was mostly supportive but very nervous," he recollects. "And one of the other investors said, 'well, you're making me nervous, but I'll support you.'" To allay their fears, the VC steered the CEO selection process very deliberately and conventionally. He retained an executive recruiter—who became so enamored of Brocade that he took his entire fee in stock. Neiman drew up a very exacting candidate profile to guide the recruiter.

"He found a long string of great candidates," the VC recounts. "You know: high profile people who knew the industry and had big-business experience. And he also turned up a guy who had run an $80 million business. He was younger, and he did not fit our profile at all." Neiman interviewed him, anyway. He liked him, but Greg Reyes was so far outside of his ideal-candidate profile that Neiman asked another partner at Crosspoint to have a discussion with him as well. "All the analytical indicators said, well, maybe we should find a better candidate. He didn't exactly fit the model. He had never been in the computer business. He had been involved in product development before, but not this kind of complex product development. But he had some analogical experience which led me to believe that he'd be able to do this. The analysis went out the window and we hired him because he was just a leader par excellence."

Before Reyes arrived in 1998, "we had been in a situation where we had a good business, but we were talking about raising another $10 million and delaying the IPO and probably losing some accounts and maybe becoming only one of several good suppliers. After Reyes took over, we never raised another nickel. We quickly realized a new business plan and reduced costs and sharpened the strategy and began to capture market share in vicious hand-to-hand combat. It was absolutely the best decision I've ever made of any kind in my entire business career."

CONCLUSION: THE COMPOSITE VC

In successful venturing, personal qualities count as much as any procedure, principle, method, or technique. But personal qualities aren't anything a venture capitalist purposefully applies. They're characteristics he or she simply possesses. They're inbred. They pop out at the birth of any Future-VC. If they're developed at all, they're developed when a mom and dad put in a good ten or twenty years' effort, with some aid from other mentors and role models along the way.

But personality, character, and human behavior can get pretty complex. It's impossible to try to probe, plumb, and adequately represent all the personal traits that intermix to create a successful venture investor. On the other hand, they're also too important to ignore. One good way to get at them is to build a fictitious, composite venture capitalist composed of the primary traits that, together, might add up to an individual who would do passably well finding and bringing up young companies.

This composite can be split into two big pieces. One piece contains the universal traits that carry over pretty consistently from successful VC to successful VC. The other part of the composite comes more from individual characteristics that show up clearly in some venture capitalists, but not universally across the whole population. They're visible only here and there, in this VC and in that

VC. No single venture capitalist possesses them all in abundance. But they're probably present at least in some degree in every VC who cracks the code to successful venturing.

A lot has already been said about the universal traits, because some of them also classify as investment methods and principles discussed in the previous chapters. When a VC exercises good judgment (Chapter Five), when he stays with a problem persistently (Chapter Eight), or when he backs up a hunch with boldness and daring (Chapter Twelve), he's calling on native abilities as much as on skills acquired and honed on the job.

But there are more than just those. In his responsibilities as recruiter for the youthful and ambitious firm Technology Crossover Ventures, partner Jake Reynolds looks to fit people into a kind of model profile of an idealized venture capitalist. It includes three primary mental bents—you might also call them intellectual approaches or even patterns of thought—that help a person negotiate the inherent demands of the trade. One is the ability to view the big picture, cutting through reams of minutia and numbing details that can cloud a complex situation. "A venture capitalist has to fly at a very high level," says Reynolds. He means viewing whole new markets and emerging businesses to develop foreknowledge of the most promising investment opportunities they may contain—all the investment opportunities, not just one or two particular ones. For example, in early 2000, as wireless communications technologies began to stir as a fertile investment bed, the big-picture view would have canvassed the field to look at wireless needs overall, coming up with maybe a handful of different technologies or services or what-have-you that would meet different essential needs in a wirelessly connected world. In a sense, in Reynolds's view, the VC is getting there before entrepreneurs do, developing a macro-investment strategy and then fitting in individual opportunities as they come along.

Second, he says, you have to be comfortable with on-the-fly decision-making. That is, operating with only surface-level information. A venture capitalist is involved in too many different projects to dissect the operations of each. "People who need to dig down and really understand all the issues are going to have a hard time being venture capitalists," he opines. "I can only know what's going on at the CEO level. I need to be told about other things. I need them documented. But I don't need to go prove them. A lot of people are not comfortable with that. They need more data."

Optimism is the last of the primary traits the VC looks for in applicants. With so much that can go wrong in a young company, a sky-is-falling fatalist may become paralyzed by indecision and fright. "You're starting with companies that are either developing new technologies, or entering markets that haven't existed before, or they're going after big competitors," illustrates Reynolds. "And you're not going to have a lot of data points to prove that this is the right place to go. It's going to take a lot of gut-feeling, and you have to have a belief that everything is going to be okay in the end." It requires not just optimism, he says, but *ultimate* optimism.

"You can't teach people those three things," says Reynolds. "Either they have them, or they do not."

But beyond such group traits, separate VCs exhibit some individual characteristics that also appear to play a pivotal role in their success. For example, in Nancy Schoendorf, the ultra optimism that Reynolds speaks of seems blended with a stubbornness that transcends mere persistence. She shows an outright unwillingness to accept failure. When she explains that she stuck with a battered portfolio company, rolling against the odds, because she always saw some dim glimmer of hope, it's clear that she saw what she looked for. Her analytical frame of mind would never have allowed her to stay involved without some discernible reason. Therefore as she peered through the murkiness she was guided by her firm intention to find at least one reason to keep the investment alive.

She says that she acquired that intensity of commitment by observing it in Jim Swartz. That points to another noteworthy trait. Call it the ability to inspire, which isn't a particularly graceful way to put it. But *charisma* isn't quite the right term, either, because it implies a charm and even a magnetism that operate more loudly than Swartz's trusting, self-assured, committed leadership that can demonstrate to colleagues that hard work pays off. If entrepreneurs running seat-of-the-pants start-ups need to perform unnatural acts to steer their companies toward success, it can't hurt them to take encouragement and learn lessons from the example of a partner, the way Schoendorf did from Swartz. "When all the other investors will walk away, Jim will pick up the pieces and out of the ashes build a successful company," she says. "He doesn't just cut and run on his deals. I think we owe a company a lot when we make an investment. When they choose us as their partner and give us equity, we're in through thick and through thin. There are times when you've got to say uncle, but we will work our butts off to make a company successful."

That's raw idealism. It counts as another individual characteristic that turns up in winning VCs.

Seth Neiman exhibits what could best be described as kindness when he protects the identity of a CEO he hustled out when Neiman determined that a company needed a more aggressive top manager. "We can tell the story if we don't embarrass anyone," he instructs. It can be tough to tell what role kindness can play in business. But it must promote greater trust. What's more, from like-minded individuals it's likely to be repaid.

Similarly, who knows if Neiman's wry, impish humor helps him bring home better investments, but it must certainly make workdays pass more easily. When recounting the history of the Pioneer Hotel Building, which is the old wooden landmark Crosspoint Venture Partners rehabbed handsomely for its headquarters, standing where Whiskey Hill Road meets Woodside Road approximately across the street from Buck's Restaurant in the tony, riding-stables town of Woodside, California, Neiman notes that the place was once a brothel. "And there are those who say it still is," he sneaks in.

Jacqueline Morby possesses a candor and directness that make deal-making with her a reassuring experience, because you feel confident in the impression she conveys. It seems impossible to mistake or mistrust her intentions. She doesn't leave you wondering what's been left out of a conversation, or what's been embellished. Morby's forthright approach can be as settling as a firm handshake with a steady-gaze eye-to-eye.

It's not quite that way with Ann Winblad, whose beguiling cleverness might make you wonder if you've played the cat, or the mouse. Her inbred asset is a sense of personal style and an accommodating grace that make you want to latch on. That quality is closer to the Pied Piper brand of charisma, which can encourage people to rally around a cause.

The troop-rallying charm of Izhar Armony derives more from his courtesy, and from the unmistakable manifestations of his deep-rooted obligation. If he keeps you waiting for a meeting, he'll at least run to the conference room to finally join you.

Donald Valentine exhibits a strong sense of entitlement that appears to grow out of a sense that he is accomplishing great things. That's pride, which is a prerequisite for accomplishing great things.

In Henry McCance, pride is tempered by diffidence. His respect and high regard for the profession seem to border at times on reverence. It seems only natural that, in order to be very good at an undertaking, a person must believe that he is engaged in something special.

But that all begins to sound like psychoanalysis, which stands far away from conventional thoughts on venture investing. Still, when you scratch beneath the surface, it is impossible to examine the success of VCs without also noting that they get a lot of help from natural tendencies like commitment, idealism, honesty, charm, pride, and reverence. These personal assets might be the real secrets of venture capital.

VENTURE CAPITAL FIRMS AND INVESTOR AND ENTREPRENEUR RESOURCES

WEB DIRECTORY

1stVenture	www.1stventure.com
21st Century Internet Venture Partners	www.21vc.com
ABN AMRO Private Equity	www.abnequity.com
Accel Partners	www.accel.com
ACI Capital Co, Inc	www.acicapital.com
Alliance Technology Ventures	www.atv.com
Alpine Technology Ventures	www.alpineventures.com
Altira Group LLC	www.altiragroup.com
Altos Ventures	www.altosvc.com
Ambrosio & Sirois	www.venture-partners.com
AmeriFinancial	www.amerifinancial.com
Amis Ventures, Inc	www.capitalyst.com
Angeles Ventures	www.angelesventures.com
Anila Corporation	www.anila.com
Apex Investment Partners	www.apexvc.com

ARCH Venture Partners	www.archventure.com
Arlington Capital Partners	www.arlingtoncap.com
Asia Pacific Ventures	www.apvco.com
AsiaTech Ventures	www.asiatechv.com
Asset Management Associates	www.assetman.com
Atlantic Coastal Ventures	www.atlanticcv.com
Atlas Venture	www.atlasventure.com
Atrium Capital	www.atriumcapital.com
Aurora Funds, Inc	www.aurorafunds.com
Austin Ventures	www.austinventures.com
Avalon Investments, Inc	www.avaloninvest.com
AVI Capital	www.avicapital.com
Bachow & Associates	www.bachow.com
Barrington Partners	www.barringtonpartners.com
Battery Ventures	www.battery.com
Beer & Partners	www.beerprt.com
Ben Franklin Technology Partners	www.benfranklin.org
Benchmark Capital	www.benchmark.com
Berkeley International Capital Corporation	www.berkeleyvc.com
Bessemer Venture Partners	www.bessemervp.com
BG Affiliates LLC	www.bgaffiliates.com
BlueStar Ventures	www.bluestarventures.com
Bodega Partners	www.bodegapartners.com
Boston Capital Ventures	www.bcv.com
Boston Millennia Partners	www.millenniapartners.com
Brentwood Venture Capital	www.brentwoodvc.com
Bridge Ventures	www.bridge-ventures.dk
Buena Venture Associates	www.buenaventure.com
Cambridge Incubator	www.cambridgeincubator.com
Cambridge Samsung Partners	www.cspartners.com

Canaan Partners	www.canaan.com
Capital Investments, Inc	www.capitalinvestmentsinc.com
CapiTech	www.hqcapitech.com
Capstone Ventures	www.capstonevc.com
The Carlyle Group	www.thecarlylegroup.com
Catalyst Investors	www.catalystinvestors.com
Catalyst Partners, Inc	www.catalystpartnersinc.com
Catalyx Group	www.catalyx.com
CCG Venture Partners	www.ccgvp.com
CEA Capital Partners	www.ceacapital.com
CeBourn, Ltd	www.cebourn.com
Charles River Ventures	www.crv.com
Charter Ventures	www.charterventures.com
Chase Capital Partners	www.chasecapital.com
ChinaVest	www.chinavest.com
CID Equity Partners	www.cidequity.com
Conru Interactive	w3.com
Coral Ventures	www.coralventures.com
CPI Ventures	www.cpiventures.com
Crosspoint Venture Partners	www.cpvp.com
Cyberspace Services	www.iplex.com/cyberspace
Delphi Ventures, Inc	www.delphiventures.com
Desco Venture Capital Group	www.descovc.com
Diamondhead Ventures	www.dhven.com
Digital Partners Venture Capital	www.digitalpartnersvc.com
Digital Technology Partners	www.dtpnet.com
Dominion Ventures, Inc	www.dominion.com
Draper Fisher Jurvetson	www.drapervc.com
Dresdner Kleinwort Benson	www.dkbprivateequity.com
DynaFund Ventures	www.dynafundventures.com
Edison Venture Fund	www.edisonventure.com
El Dorado Ventures	www.eldoradoventures.com

Embryon Capital	www.embryon.com
Equity Ventures Ltd	www.ventures.demon.co.uk
Euclid Partners	www.euclidpartners.com
Explorador net	www.explorador.net
Fairfax Partners II	www.fairfaxpartners.com
FDG Associates	www.fdgassociates.com
Fidelity Ventures	www.fidelityventures.com
Flatiron Partners	www.flatironpartners.com
Focus Capital Group	www.fcg.co.il
Galen Partners	www.galen-partners.com
Geocapital Partners	www.geocapital.com
Great Hill Partners, LLC	www.greathillpartners.com
Greenhouse for Startups	www.greenhouseforstartups.com
Greylock	www.greylock.com
Grimaldi Group, The	www.thegrimaldigroup.com
Grotech Capital Group	www.grotech.com
Grove Strategic Ventures	www.gsv.com
GSM Capital	www.gsmcapital.com
H&Q Venture Associates	www.hqva.com
Harris & Harris Group	www.hhgp.com
Highland Capital Partners	www.hcp.com
Hudson Venture Partners, LP	www.hudsonptr.com
Hummer Winblad Venture Partners	www.humwin.com
Huron Capital Partners	www.huroncapital.com
Impact Venture Partners	www.impactvp.com
Innovation Factory, The	www.innovationfactory.com
Integral Captial Partners	www.integralcapital.com
Interactive Minds	www.iminds.com
Internet Finance Partners	www.ifp.com
Internet Venture Group	www.ivgcorp.com
Intersouth Partners	www.intersouth.com
InterWest Partners	www.interwest.com

Jefferson Capital Partners, Ltd	www.jeffersoncapital.com
Katalyst Net Acceleration	www.katalyst.com
Kestrel Venture Management	www.kestrelvm.com
Keystone Venture Capital Management Co	www.keystoneventures.com
Kleiner Perkins Caufield & Byers	www.kpcb.com
Korea Technology Finance Corporation	www.kdbcapital.co.kr
L&H Investment Company	www.lhsl.com
Levine Leichtman Capital Partners	www.llcp.com
Levy Trajman Management Investment Inc	www.ltmi.com
LF Venture Capital	www.lfvc.com
Lightspeed Venture Partners	www.lightspeedvp.com
Longworth Venture Partners	www.longworth.com
Lovett Miller & Co	www.lovettmiller.com
M&A Capital Group	www.macapitalgroup.com
Mason Wells	www.masonwells.com
Massey Burch Capital Corp	www.masseyburch.com
Matrix Partners	www.matrixpartners.com
Medicus Venture Partners	www.medicusvc.com
Menlo Ventures	www.menloventures.com
Mentor Capital Partners	www.mentorcapitalpartners.com
Mericom	www.meri.com
Mitsui USA Private Equity Group	www.mitsuipe.com
Mohr, Davidow Ventures	www.mdv.com
Moodenbaugh Media Corporation	www.moodenbaugh.com
Morgenthaler	www.morgenthaler.com

Myne Corporation	www.myne.com
Nassau Capital	www.nassau.com
NEA—New Enterprise Associates	www.nea.com
New Generation Holdings, Inc	www.ngpx.com
Newbury Ventures	www.newburyven.com
North Bridge Venture Partners	www.nbvp.com
Norwest Venture Capital	www.norwestvc.com
Nth Power Technologies, Inc	www.nthfund.com
Oak Investment Partners	www.oakinv.com
OffRoad Capital	www.offroadcapital.com
Olympic Venture Partners	www.ovp.com
Onset Ventures	www.onset.com
Opus Capital	www.opuscapital.com
Oresa Ventures	www.oresaventures.com
Pacific Link Investment Group	www.plventure.com
Pacific Venture Group	www.pacven.com
Pan American Global Group, Inc	www.panamglobal.com
Patricof & Co Ventures, Inc	www.patricof.com
Pennell Venture Partners	nell.com
Pennsylvania Early Stage Partners	www.paearlystage.com
Pinetree Capital	www.pinetreecapital.com
Pinnacle West Capital Corp.	www.pinnaclewest.com/home.asp
Platinum Venture Partners, Inc	www.divineinterventures.com
Point West Ventures	www.pointwestventures.com
Polaris Venture Partners	www.polarisventures.com
Prometheus Partners, LP	www.prometheuspartners.com
Prospect Street Ventures	www.prospectstreet.com

Providence Equity Partners	www.provequity.com
Psilos	www.psilos.com
Redleaf Venture Management	www.redleaf.com
Rein Capital	www.reincapital.com
Reuters Greenhouse Fund	www.rvcco.com
Rosewood Capital	www.rosewoodvc.com
Rothschild Quantico Capital	www.quantico.com
RRE Investors, LLC	www.rre.com
Rubicon Capital Investments	www.rubcap.com
RWI Group	www.rwigroup.com
Sacramento Area Venture Capital Network	www.sacareavcnetwork.com
San Francisco Venture Enterprises	www.sfve.com
Sentinel Capital Partners	www.sentinelpartners.com
Sequoia Capital	www.sequoiacap.com
Sevin Rosen Funds	www.srfunds.com
The Shepherd Group	www.tsgequity.com
SI Ventures	www.siventures.com
Sierra Ventures	www.sierraven.com
Silicon Alley Capital Management	www.siliconalleycapital.com
Silicon Valley Capital Network	www.jointventure.org
Siparex Group	www.siparex.com
Skypoint Capital Corporation	www.skypointcorp.com
Snider Capital, LP	www.snidercapital.com
Softbank Technology Ventures	www.sbvc.com
Springboard plc	www.springboard-vm.co.uk

The Sprout Group	www.sproutgroup.com
SSM Ventures	www.ssmventures.com
St. Paul Venture Capital	www.stpaulvc.com
Sternhill Partners	www.sternhillpartners.com
Stoller & Associates	www.stollerassociates.com
Summit Partners	www.summitpartners.com
Sutter Hill Ventures	www.shv.com
Svoboda, Collins LLC	www.svoco.com
TA Associates	www.ta.com
Technologieholding	www.technologieholding.de
Technology Crossover Ventures	www.tcv.com
Technology Management and Funding	www.tmflp.com
Technology Partners	www.technologypartners.com
Technology Venture Partners	www.tvp.com
Thoma Cressey Equity Partners	www.tc.nu
Tribune Ventures	www.tribune.com/ventures
Trident Capital, LP	www.tridentcap.com
Trinity Venture Capital	www.trinity-vc.ie
Trinity Ventures	www.trinityventures.com
U S Venture Partners (USVP)	www.usvp.com
Union Atlantic LC	www.ualc.com
Vanguard Venture Partners	www.vanguardventures.com
VenGlobal Capital	www.venglobal.com
Venrock Associates	www.venrock.com
Venture Capital Report Ltd	www.vcr1978.com
Venture Highway	www.venturehighway.com
Venture Innovations, Inc	www.venturenetworking.com
The Venture Site	www.venturesite.co.uk
Venture Strategy Group	www.venturestrategy.com
VentureOne	www.v1.com

Vestar Capital Partners	www.vestarcapital.com
VisionQuest Technology Ventures	www.visionquestvc.com
VistaWEB	www.vistaweb.com
Walden Venture Capital	www.waldenvc.com
Waterside Capital Corporation	www.watersidecapital.com
Waud Capital Partners	www.waudcapital.com
Weiss, Peck & Greer Venture Partners	www.waudcapital.com
WENR Corporation	www.wenr.net
Whimsical Holdings, Inc	www.whimsical.net
Willis Stein & Partners	www.willisstein.com
Windward Ventures	www.windwardventures.com
Winston Financial Group, Inc	www.winfin.com
Worldview Technology Partners	www.worldview.com
Xenva Ltd	www.xenva.com
Yellowstone Capital, Inc	www.yellowstonecapital.com

INDEX